Cognitive-Behavioral Methods for Social Workers

A WORKBOOK

—————————▼▲▼—————————

JACQUELINE CORCORAN

Virginia Commonwealth University

PEARSON

Boston   New York   San Francisco
Mexico City   Montreal   Toronto   London   Madrid   Munich   Paris
Hong Kong   Singapore   Tokyo   Cape Town   Sydney

Editor-in-Chief: Karen Hanson
Series Editor: Patricia Quinlin
Editorial Assistant: Sara Holliday
Marketing Manager: Laura Lee Manley
Manufacturing Buyer: JoAnne Sweeney
Cover Coordinator: Joel Gendron
Production Coordinator: Pat Torelli Publishing Services
Editorial-Production Service: Stratford Publishing Services, Inc.
Electronic Composition: Stratford Publishing Services, Inc.

For related titles and support materials, visit our online catalog at www.ablongman.com.

Between the time Web site information is gathered and then published, it is not unusual for some sites to have closed. Also, the transcription of URLs can result in unintended typographical errors. The publisher would appreciate notification where these errors occur so that they may be corrected in subsequent editions.

Library of Congress Cataloging-in-Publication Data
Corcoran, Jacqueline.
    Cognitive-behavioral methods for social workers : a workbook / Jacqueline Corcoran.
        p.   cm.
    Includes bibliographical references.
    ISBN 0-205-42379-5
        1. Social work education.   I. Title.

HV11.C71874 2006
361.3'2—dc22   2005050912

Printed in the United States of America

10 9 8 7 6 5 4 3 2 1   09 08 07 06 05

To Alexa Sian
&
Miles Rhys

Contents

—▾▲▾—

Preface

——— ▾▲▾ ———

The purpose of *Cognitive-Behavioral Methods for Social Workers: A Workbook* is to build social work students' and practitioners' knowledge and skills on the use of cognitive-behavioral interventions. Cognitive-behavioral therapy is a broad class of present-focused interventions with a shared focus on changing *cognition* (thoughts, beliefs, and assumptions about the world), changing *behavior*, and building clients' *coping skills*. Behavior theory is concerned with how human behavior, whether adaptive or problematic, is developed, sustained, or eliminated through its external *reinforcement*. Cognitive theory focuses on the rationality of one's thinking patterns and the connections between thoughts, feelings, and behaviors. The nature of change in cognitive-behavioral therapy is apparent in its hyphenated name; both behavior theory and cognitive theory are subsumed in the approach.

Cognitive-behavioral theory is a major practice theory taught in many foundational and advanced direct practice courses in masters of social work programs. However, this book can also be used for students in undergraduate programs and is designed for social workers in all kinds of settings (in other words, not limited to those in which only therapy is practiced). The workbook format with brief explanations, plenty of examples, and exercises makes the concepts and applications easy to understand.

Cognitive-Behavioral Methods for Social Workers: A Workbook presents instructional material on how to use cognitive-behavioral therapy throughout the helping process: assessment; goal formulation and planning; intervention; and evaluation. The student gains knowledge and skills by working on case examples illustrated in the workbook. Case examples cover the range of different settings, client problems, and client populations that social workers may see. Many of these case vignettes are excerpted from actual students' work, and the students are acknowledged for their contribution. Other cases are composites. All cases have been de-identified in terms of names of clients, staff, agencies, location, and other details.

Students are asked to assess cases in which principles of cognitive-behavior therapy and techniques were misapplied and how methods could have been used more effectively. Answers are supplied in an instructor's manual. Space is provided in the workbook so that students can apply the instructional material to their own practice. Through these case applications, students can demonstrate their knowledge and skills in assessing, planning, and implementing cognitive-behavioral interventions.

Another section of the book involves managing barriers, such as lack of motivation and compliance. Principles and basic interventions from motivational interviewing is included. Because cognitive-behavioral therapy has been criticized as deficit-focused (Greene, Lee, Trask, & Rheinscheld, 1996) and social work prides itself on a focus on strengths, cognitive-behavioral methods are taught from a strengths-based perspective. Specifically, goals and target behaviors are defined and tracked as the presence of positive behaviors rather than the absence of negative behaviors, and students are taught how to enlarge upon client strengths to combat the "irrational" thinking that is so much a focus of cognitive-behavioral therapy.

Cognitive-Behavioral Methods for Social Workers: A Workbook also ties in with the movement in social work toward evidence-based practice. Increasingly, social workers are held to standards of accountability in which they are called upon to practice with methods that have been supported by the best available evidence. Social workers have a responsibility to their clients to intervene with the most effective theoretical methods possible, methods that have been tested and that have proven clinical utility. This guideline for social work practice has been promulgated both in the National Association of Social Workers Code of Ethics (1999) and in the Council on Social Work Education Curriculum Policy Statement (2004).

In reviews involving different problem areas, cognitive-behavioral therapy has been empirically validated. These problem areas include pain management (Compas, Haaga, Keefe, Leitenberg, & Williams, 1998), anger (Beck & Fernandez, 1998), depression (Dobson, 1989; Gaffan, Tsaousis, & Kemp-Wheeler, 1995; Gerson, Belin, Kaufman, Mintz, & Jarvik, 1999), anxiety (Bakker, van Balkom, Spinhoven, & Blaauw, 1998; Feske & Chambless, 1995; Gould, Otto, &

Pollack, 1995), substance abuse and dependence (DeRubeis & Crits-Christoph, 1998; Irvin, Bowers, Dunn, & Wang, 1999), bulimia nervosa (Whittal, Agras, & Gould, 1999), and schizophrenia (Pilling, Bebbington, Kuipers, Garety, Geddes, Orbach, & Morgan, 2002). Cognitive-behavioral therapy also has proven efficacy with marital (Dunn & Schwebel, 1995) and family problems (Corcoran, 2000), and externalizing and internalizing problems in youth (Kazdin & Weisz, 1998). These problems are present in the diversity of settings in which social workers are placed or employed—child welfare, family support programs, hospitals, schools, clubhouses for the mentally ill, programs for individuals with mental retardation, nursing homes, hospice, just to name a few. Knowledge of cognitive-behavioral methods is useful in many of these contexts so that you, as the practitioner, are better prepared to alleviate client suffering and improve functioning.

Another aspect of evidence-based practice involves social workers' facility and competence in evaluating their own practice with individual clients (Cournoyer & Powers, 2002). Since one of the fundamental principles of cognitive-behavioral intervention is evaluation of methods, this workbook also devotes a section to helping students construct scales and single-system designs to evaluate their work with individual client systems.

To summarize, *Cognitive-Behavioral Methods for Social Workers: A Workbook* offers the following benefits to readers:

- Familiarity with cognitive-behavioral therapy, an evidence-based practice approach that has been validated for many types of problem areas.
- A systematic, methodical, and applied approach to teaching and learning cognitive-behavioral skills.
- Case examples from a range of practice settings and client problems and populations to show students how they can adapt techniques to the situations social workers may encounter.
- Understanding of how to evaluate and assess client outcomes.
- An appendix of cognitive-behavioral manuals and self-help books have been included for the reader's use.

References

----------▼▲▼----------

Bakker, A., van Balkom, A., Spinhoven, P., & Blaauw, B. (1998). Follow-up on the treatment of panic disorder with or without agoraphobia: A quantitative review. *Journal of Nervous & Mental Disease, 186,* 414–419.

Beck, R., & Fernandez, E. (1998). Cognitive-behavioral therapy in the treatment of anger: A meta-analysis. *Cognitive Therapy and Research, 22,* 63–74.

Compas, B., Haaga, D., Keefe, F., Leitenberg, H., & Williams, D. (1998). Sampling of empirically supported psychological treatments from health psychology: Smoking, chronic pain, cancer, and bulimia nervosa. *Journal of Consulting and Clinical Psychology, 66,* 89–112.

Corcoran, J. (2000). *Evidence-based social work practice with families: A lifespan approach.* New York: Springer.

Council on Social Work Education. (2004). Curriculum policy statement for master's degree programs in social work education. Alexandria, VA: Author.

Cournoyer, B., & Powers, G. (2002). Evidence-based social work: The quiet revolution continues. In A. Roberts & G. Greene (Eds.), *Social workers' desk reference* (pp. 798–807). New York: Oxford University Press.

DeRubeis, R., & Crits-Christoph, P. (1998). Empirically supported individual and group psychological treatments for adult mental disorders, *Journal of Consulting and Clinical Psychology, 66,* 37–52.

Dobson, K. S. (1989). A meta-analysis of the efficacy of cognitive therapy for depression. *Journal of Consulting and Clinical Psychology, 57,* 414–419.

Dunn, R., & Schwebel, A. (1995). Meta-analytic review of marital therapy outcome research. *Journal of Family Psychology, 9,* 58–68.

Feske, U., & Chambless, D. (1995). Cognitive behavioral versus exposure only treatment for social phobia: A meta-analysis. *Behavior Therapy, 26,* 695–720.

Gaffan, E., Tsaousis, I., & Kemp-Wheeler, S. (1995). Researcher allegiance and meta-analysis: The case of cognitive therapy for depression. *Journal of Consulting and Clinical Psychology, 63,* 966–980.

Gerson, S., Belin, T., Kaufman, A., Mintz, J., & Jarvik, L. (1999). Pharmacological and psychological treatments for depressed older patients: A meta-analysis and overview of recent findings. *Harvard Review of Psychiatry, 7*, 1–28.

Gould, R., Otto, M., & Pollack, M. (1995). A meta-analysis of treatment outcome for panic disorder. *Clinical Psychology Review, 15*, 819–844.

Greene, G. J., Lee, M. Y., Trask, R., & Rheinscheld, J. (1996). Client strengths and crisis intervention: A solution-focused approach. *Crisis Intervention, 3*, 43–63.

Irvin, J., Bowers, C., Dunn, M., & Wang, M. (1999). Efficacy of relapse prevention: A meta-analytic review. *Journal of Consulting & Clinical Psychology, 67*, 563–570.

Kazdin, A., & Weisz, J. (1998). Identifying and developing empirically supported child and adolescent treatments. *Journal of Consulting and Clinical Psychology, 66*, 19–36.

National Association of Social Workers. (1999). *Code of ethics.* Revised and adopted by the delegate assembly of the National Association of Social Workers. Washington, DC: NASW Press.

Pilling, S., Bebbington, P., Kuipers, E., Garety, P., Geddes, J., Orbach, G., & Morgan, C. (2002). Psychological treatments in schizophrenia: I. Meta-analysis of family intervention and cognitive behaviour therapy. *Psychological Medicine, 32*, 763–782.

Whittal, M., Agras, W., & Gould, R. (1999). Bulimia nervosa: A meta-analysis of psychosocial and pharmacological treatments. *Behavior Therapy, 30*, 117–135.

Acknowledgments

——————— ▼▲▼ ———————

I would like to extend grateful acknowledgment to the following students and colleagues for their contributions.

Students: Carrie Becker, Caroline Daimler, Sarah Davis, Margie Duran-Freeman, Krisha Hodges, Liat Katz, Lori Kopp, Sheri Mintz, Beth Norris, Jessica Pane, Grace Stapleton, Candace Strother, Dana Taylor, Angela Williams, Keri Williams, and Jennifer Woozley.

Colleagues: Theresa Early, David Springer, and Joseph Walsh.

My appreciation also goes to the following reviewers for their helpful comments on the manuscript: Robert Bennett, Indiana University; Sarah S. Bradley, Portland State University; Michael Paul Melendez, Simmons College; and Mary P. Van Hook, University of Central Florida.

1

— ▼▲▼ —

Behavioral Assessment, Goal Formulation, and Evaluation

During the assessment process, the social worker helps the client understand his or her problems in terms of their specific and concrete manifestations. Information is gathered about the environmental conditions (cues) that produce the behavior and the consequences that follow. It must be noted that during this information-gathering process, the social worker has to listen empathically to clients' concerns, reflecting the content of their messages as well as their underlying feelings. In this way rapport is built, and people feel heard and understood. A foundation of support, trust, and safety has to be established at the start so that the client is willing not only to share information but also to learn new behaviors.

Behavioral Definition of the Problem

Clients often speak in general terms about a recurrent problem ("we're always arguing"). In response, the social worker should ask questions to elicit behavioral details: "To help me get a better sense of what happens when you argue, tell me what happened the last time this occurred. Where were you? What was going on?" When you ask a client for an example, it can involve a typical incident, the most recent, or the most severe. To get at the behavioral specifics, the following questions can be asked (Bertolino & O'Hanlon, 2002):

- What do you do when you experience the behavior?
- When do you experience it?
- Where?
- How long does the problem typically last?
- What bodily reactions do you experience?
- How long do these reactions last?
- How often does the problem typically happen (once an hour, once a day, once a week)?
- What is its typical timing (time of day, week, month, year)?
- What do the people around you usually do when the problem is happening?

EXAMPLE 1-1

This example demonstrates how the social worker cannot just accept at face value global statements clients may make. Instead, the social worker must explore the concrete behaviors that underlie client descriptions.

A social work intern at an HIV clinic worked with Sonya, a Hispanic mother of two girls, ages 11 and 8, and a 6-year-old boy. Sonya had a live-in boyfriend who was absent much of the time because of his work schedule. Sonya was having particular problems with her 8-year-old girl, Ellie. Sonya used terms such as "bad child," "mean," and "vindictive" to describe Ellie. The social work intern probed for specifics by asking, "What is Ellie doing when she's being bad?" Sonya explained that Ellie won't obey any commands she gives her, such as to come inside to do her homework or to stop playing and do her chores. Sonya's main concern was that Ellie had recently become more violent, hitting, biting, and kicking her siblings.

Another way to gather information about the problem is to have people complete standardized questionnaires (also called measures, scales, inventories, and instruments). Measures have been developed for many different problems and help to determine the existence of certain behaviors, attitudes, feelings, or qualities—and their intensity or severity. Measures have been *standardized* when they have been tested (normed) on a relevant group of people, a process that results in psychometric data, specifically information about reliability and validity, that has to meet certain acceptable standards. Reliability refers to the consistency and accuracy of the measure; validity involves the extent to which an instrument measures what it purports to measure. For the different methods of determining reliability and validity, please see a research text (e.g., Rubin & Babbie, 2005). Some guidelines for having clients complete measurement instruments follow:

Select a measure. Selection of particular measures to use may be determined by the particular program a client attends or the client's presenting problem.

Provide a rationale. A justification to provide to clients for using a measure is that it is a quick way to get information that will assist the social worker in better understanding how to help. It will also help track progress if the measurement instrument is completed over time.

Explain how to fill out the form. Read aloud the directions, which includes how the client should respond to items. In the explanation, assure clients that there are no right or wrong answers.

Answer questions, clarify, look the form over. It is important to assess clients' literacy level, whether they are children or adults. If necessary, read each question and response to the client. If clients are unsure of an answer, they should be encouraged to provide what they think is the "best" answer. Social workers should avoid interpreting the items or questions. The social worker should check over the measure after it is completed, looking for items left blank and response-set bias (e.g., giving all items a 5 in a 5-point scale).

Score the measure. Ideally, measures should be scored when the client is present so that immediate feedback can be given.

Repeat the measure at a later date. Using the same measure one or more times (or every time if you are carrying out a single-subject design, discussed later in this chapter) provides both the client and the worker with an assessment of change. This is an important step in motivating clients, solidifying gains they have made through the therapeutic process, and documenting outcomes for accountability purposes.

Exercise 1–1

The following exercise can increase your ability to ask about behavioral specifics. For each statement, decide what questions you would ask to get at the behavioral manifestations of the problem. From your knowledge of people, or by asking a classmate to role play the client, create some hypothetical indicators of the problem behavior.

1. A parent describes her child as having attention deficit/hyperactivity disorder (ADHD).

2. A client who is having problems with his supervisor describes her as a "very angry, controlling person."

3. Your classmate describes a client she is having trouble with as "defiant, having aggressive outbursts, and having difficulty managing her anger."

4. A client says about herself, "I'm a very selfish person."

5. Your field instructor refers to a client as "borderline" and "manipulative."

Exercise 1-2

Recall one trait that you use to describe yourself or another person in your life. Break that trait down into its behavioral manifestations. How does this change your perception of that trait?

Exercise 1-3

This exercise shows you that your sense of optimism about the possibility of change might depend on whether clients are described in global terms or their behaviors are defined operationally.

1. What seems more easily changed: an "oppositional" child or that child's talking back and refusing to do tasks when parents or teachers so request?

2. What seems more easily changed: a child who, according to his mother, has ADHD or that child's behavior of not completing homework?

3. What seems more easily changed: a child whose mother describes her as "cold" or the behavior of not telling her mother how she feels?

Cues and Consequences

After breaking behaviors down into their concrete manifestations, the social worker continues the assessment by asking about the cues (also called antecedents and triggers) for the behavior ("What starts it?"). This process helps clients gain more awareness of their behaviors, what led up to them, and how they are being reinforced. Many people with problem behaviors often view them as "coming out of the blue" or "just happening" (e.g., "suddenly, I'll just explode," "I find myself screaming at my partner, and I don't know how I got there," "I felt like having a drink, so I had one"). However, there are sequences of events that lead up to problem behaviors. If a person is made more aware of these events, he or she will have a way of anticipating, avoiding, or coping with these events.

One technique that makes it easier for some people to understand the sequences that lead up to problem behavior involves a scale from 1 to 10 in which 10 is the ultimate expression of the problem behavior (e.g., the drink or the temper tantrum). Starting at the lower end of the scale, you ask clients to go through the scale and identify their escalating triggers. Sometimes the client must trace the sequences of the particular day, starting at the beginning, so he or she can see how the problem behavior built up over the course of that day.

EXAMPLE 1-2

Lila is a Hispanic mother of four children who is under child protective services investigation for physical abuse of her children. The social worker in this instance used the scale to help Lila identify what built up to the recent incident of physical abuse.

With the social worker's prompting, Lila described the following cues associated with each number on the scale:

1. "Feeling tired, not getting enough sleep from the night before because the kids wouldn't go to bed."
2. "Being mad with them for not getting dressed when I said so."
4. "Because they wouldn't listen, we were late for their immunization appointment at the doctor's office. If they didn't get the shots, I wouldn't be able to enroll them in school."

5. "The kids were acting out in the doctor's office, and I felt hot and embarrassed as everyone was watching us. I imagined everyone was thinking I didn't have any control over my children and that they were brats."

6. "By the time we got home, I was drained from listening to them argue all the way home."

7. "I got a phone call from a friend and just when I was beginning to relax, the kids started hitting each other, screaming, and crying. My stomach was in knots, and I was thinking about how they always ruined everything."

9. "I was screaming at them. I just had it."

10. "I got out my belt and just began lashing out at all of them."

As this example demonstrates (see Figure 1–1), the scaling exercise increases understanding of the sequences leading up to the problem behavior. It is not necessary for clients to pinpoint each number on the scale, but the notion of sequences escalating to 10 provides the sense that problem behaviors don't just happen out of nowhere. There are physical, cognitive, social, emotional, and environmental cues that mount to contribute to the behavior.

One domain that might need further attention involves the affective domain, or the client's feelings. Although behavioral approaches tend to deemphasize feelings, discussion of client's feelings are very important. First,

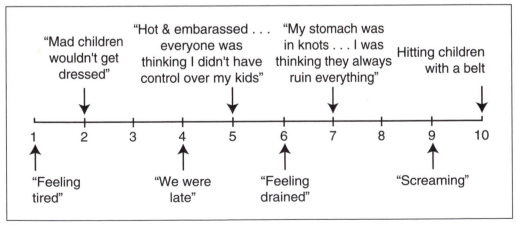

Figure 1–1

conveying understanding of feelings can build the supportive alliance that is necessary for change to occur. Second, feelings are often triggers for unproductive action. For instance, a person is scared and decides to threaten others to feel safer; a person who is bored may be more prone to use drugs. However, people are often unaware of the feelings that trigger them to act in certain ways. Therefore, building people's awareness of their feelings and the behaviors that follow gives them important information that they are having some difficulty managing certain emotions. The social worker can then target interventions that will facilitate clients' coping in more productive ways.

Another important category of questions asks about the consequences of the behavior ("What happens afterward?"). This information helps both the social worker and the client gain a sense of what is reinforcing about the behavior (see Chapter 2) or the detrimental consequences that can be used to build the client's motivation to change (see Chapter 9).

Figure 1–2 shows the five domains (social, environmental, emotionally, cognitive, and physical) in which both cues for the behavior and its consequences may occur (Carroll, 1998). Table 1–1 includes a comprehensive list of inquiries the social worker can make about the cues and consequences in each of these five domains. A cues and consequences worksheet provides a template for use by clients or the social worker. Ideally, the social worker should write out the assessment, because critical information is gathered at this stage, then used to generate goals and an intervention plan.

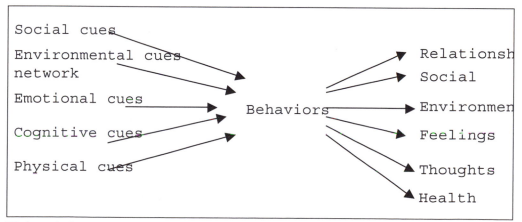

Figure 1–2

TABLE 1–1 Questions on Cues and Consequences

Domain	Antecedents (Triggers, Cues)	Consequences (Reinforcers)
Social	With whom does the client spend most of his or her time?	How has the client's social network changed since the problem began or escalated?
	Does the client have relationships with people who do not have the problem?	How have his or her relationships been affected?
	Does the client live with someone who is involved in the problem?	
Environmental	What are the particular environmental cues for the problem?	What people, places, and things have been affected by the problem?
	What is the level of the client's day-to-day exposure to these cues?	Has the client's environment changed as a result of the problem?
	Can some of these cues be easily avoided?	
Emotional	What feeling states precede the occurrence of the problem?	How does the client feel afterward?
		How does the client feel about himself or herself?
Cognitive	What thoughts run through the client's mind?	What does the client think afterward?
	What beliefs does he or she have about the problem?	What does the client say to himself or herself?

TABLE 1–1 (*Continued*)

Domain	Antecedents (Triggers, Cues)	Consequences (Reinforcers)
Physical	What uncomfortable physical states precede the problem?	How does the client feel physically afterward? What is his or her physical health like as a result?

Table 1–2 goes on to provide an example of a behavioral assessment (both the cues and the consequences) for Jennifer, a client involved with the child protective services system because of neglect of her children. The neglect stemmed largely from Jennifer's alcohol and crack cocaine addictions; therefore, the assessment focuses on her substance abuse.

TABLE 1–2   **Case Example of a Behavioral Assessment**

Domain	Antecedents (Triggers, Cues)	Consequences (Reinforcers)
Social	She lives in a crime-infested, low-income, urban community and often sees people she knows who use drugs.	Her relationship with her family has suffered. She has neglected her children (leaving them alone while she "parties" and spending money on drugs rather than on necessities for the children). She avoids her mother and sisters, who disapprove of her lifestyle. When she does see them, she gets in arguments with them because she has borrowed money without repaying it and often leaves her children with them without saying where she is.

TABLE 1–2 (*Continued*)

Domain	Antecedents (Triggers, Cues)	Consequences (Reinforcers)
Environmental	Being short on money when the rent is due and feels stressed. To relieve stress, uses drugs and alcohol.	Money problems worsen; she has spent money on drugs and alcohol and now has to pay escalating late fees as well as the rent.
Emotional	Drug use to relieve feelings of depression about the state of her life: rift with her mother and sisters, neglect of children, involvement in child protective services system.	She feels increased despair over the state of her life and what she is doing to her children.
Cognitive	"The only thing that will make me feel better is to use drugs."	"I did it again. I can't stop. I'm a bad mother."
Physical	Craving, restlessness, agitation.	Hungover, respiratory problems from smoking crack cocaine.

Exercise 1-4

This exercise will build your familiarity with assessing cues and consequences for a problem behavior and its consequences. Take a problem behavior of your own or someone who is willing to be interviewed by you. Using the worksheet provided, go through the various domains for both the cues and consequences.

WORKSHEET **1–1 Cues and Consequences**

Domain	Cues	Consequences
Social		
Environmental		
Emotional		

WORKSHEET 1–1 (*Continued*)

Cognitive		
Physical		

Goals

From the process of conducting a behavioral assessment, the specific nature of the problem and the reinforcers and triggers that keep the problem in operation are determined. From here, the social worker and client together construct concrete target behaviors as goals, giving close attention to the antecedent conditions and contingencies required to bring about the desired new behaviors. This section focuses on general guidelines for goal setting and explores ways to measure progress. Evaluation is discussed because it is tied to goal formulation and tracking goals. However, it is recognized that evaluation continues throughout the helping process and determines when the process ends.

The guidelines for goal setting include the following:

1. *Explain the rationale for goals.*
   - To provide focus to the work.
   - To get social worker and client agreement about what should be done.
   - To monitor progress of the intervention.
   - To know when the work is complete (Hepworth, Rooney, & Larsen, 2002).

2. *For people who don't want to change, start where the client is.* In a number of different practice settings, social workers see clients who have been mandated to receive services, whereas cognitive-behavioral intervention is typically for those who are sufficiently motivated to learn and practice new strategies. Therefore, it is sometimes necessary to work on building motivation before a person is ready for cognitive-behavioral intervention (Carroll, 1998). The basics of motivational interviewing are described in Chapter 9. Other ways to engage the nonvoluntary client are through solution-focused questions that ask clients what they need to do to address the demands of the referral source. "What do you think you need to do so you don't have to come here anymore?" "What will convince your probation officer [or other authority figure such as a parent or judge] that you don't need to talk to me anymore?" (Berg & Miller, 1992). Typically, people give general, vague responses: "When I'm good." The facilitator's job is to help the client come up with concrete, observable indicators (Cade & O'Hanlon, 1993). "What will you be doing differently when you are good?"

This question not only helps clarify for clients what it is they have to work on ("Go to school, I guess, and be home when I'm supposed to") and facilitates goal setting, it also helps clients realize the social worker is not invested in their continued presence in treatment and is willing to work with them to that end.

3. *Reframe a goal so that it is within the client's control and works with the system that is most amenable to change.* Often, a person may want another person to change (a partner, child, other family member, coworker, supervisor, neighbor, friend). You, as the social worker, can explain that you cannot make a person outside the helping relationship become different. However, clients can influence the behavior of another by changing their own actions.

One common example involves parents of children who need help of some kind. Parents often want their children to be seen alone by the social worker rather than be involved themselves. A way to engage parents in this process is to stress to them their importance to their children ("You are much more important to your child than I will ever be. If I can help you deal with your child and you do this at home, you will be much further along"). Parents can also be told about the cognitive abilities of young children, that they have a difficult time generalizing behavior learned in one setting to another. Therefore, if parents are present in session and see the new skills their children are learning, these effects can be carried over to the home. In particular, for treatment of externalizing behaviors in children, research shows that the most effective approaches involve parent training and other family interventions (Brestan & Eyberg, 1998; Serketich & Dumas, 1996).

Another common example involves people who get help so that their partners will return to them.

EXAMPLE 1-3

Mikhael, a Russian immigrant to the United States, has been divorced from his wife for 3 years. When asked about his goals, Mikhael said that he wanted to get back with his wife. The social work student said they couldn't "make" his ex-wife feel or act any differently toward him. However, Mikhael had frequent contact with her to manage visitation and parenting responsibilities. He therefore had opportunities to show his ex-wife that he himself could behave differently. The student suggested that they work on managing his anger and learning new communication skills so that he and his ex-wife could talk about the children and negotiate more effectively. The social work student said she didn't know whether his ex-wife would ever get back with him; but if a reconciliation were possible, Mikhael's ex-wife would first need to see that he had changed his behavior.

4. *Individualize goals rather than rely on agency-generated goals.* In some agencies, case plans involve listing the dysfunctions clients bring and then assigning them rote goals and services. For instance, a child welfare client who was using substances when her child was neglected receives substance abuse treatment; an incident of family violence warrants a perpetrator group (Christensen, Todahl, & Barrett, 1999). This practice leaves out client input. If a goal is not personally important to a client, he or she will not be motivated to pursue it. Goals should be related as much as possible to what a client sees as the problem.

5. *Goals should be considered in terms of final outcome rather than the formal services in which clients participate* (Christensen et al., 1999). For instance, rather than "attending a parenting skills group," the goal should focus on what the parent is expected to achieve as a result of attending the group. This helps both social worker and client develop a mind-set toward outcome rather than simply going through the motions of attending different services. Some clients might feel understandably overwhelmed or intimidated by the prospect of participating in a multitude of services and classes. If efforts are instead centered on final results, they can clearly see what they are working toward and might be more motivated to get there.

6. *Formulate a minimum number of goals.* When clients enter into the helping process, they are often overwhelmed by many simultaneous stressors, such as divorce, death of a family member, a family move, financial problems, health problems, behavior problems in children, and more. Focusing on a limited number of goals is critical, since the client needs to achieve success and experience some confidence as a result of his or her efforts. If efforts are scattered

around many diverse goals, chances are likely that the client may not achieve success in any one area.

Therefore, goals must be prioritized with the client's input: "Which of these goals is most important for you to center on? Which one would make the most difference to you right now?" Of course, the social worker may offer input into which of the goals might make the most difference. For instance, goals having to do with safety (getting a protective order, severing contact with an abusive partner) would be of foremost priority and might assist the progress of other goals, such as bolstering mood and improving behavior of children in the household.

The social worker may also offer input when noticing behaviors that crosscut domains of the client's life in which difficulty is experienced. For example, a client may report anger problems at work, with children, and with a partner. A possible goal in this situation is to work on improving communication skills and managing anger.

Individuals already experiencing a multitude of life stressors, including poverty, lack of adequate housing, neighborhood violence, and so forth, will not be able to scatter their efforts and seek services from numerous agencies in the community at once (Azar & Wolfe, 1998).

7. *Some goals may have to be partialized,* broken down into smaller subgoals or tasks. For example, in order for a woman to meet the goal of leaving an abusive partner, she might first have to attain several subgoals, such as getting job training and finding employment in order to become financially independent; she might have to arrange transportation so that she can attend training and get to a job; she might have to find reliable and safe child care for her children. Such subgoals in themselves require great effort and represent major achievements.

8. *Goals should be feasible considering baseline behaviors.* For example, if a child's conduct in school is rated as unsatisfactory every day of the week, then a goal of five satisfactory days would be out of his reach. Perhaps an achievable beginning goal instead might be two satisfactory days.

9. *State goals as the presence of positive behaviors rather than the absence of negative behaviors.* This keeps the focus on what the client wants rather than on what he or she doesn't want. For instance, rather than being stated as "Stop talking back at school," the goal should be phrased as "Follow directions" or

"Work quietly in the classroom." To get the client thinking within this frame, the question can be asked: "What will you be doing instead of [the problem behavior]?" The social worker must be persistent, since clients often continue to talk about the absence of negatives (e.g., "I don't know—he just won't be talking back."). This tendency, however, keeps the focus on negative behavior rather than on desired behavior.

10. *Goals should be delineated in behaviorally specific ways.* When a specific behavior or action is attached to the goal, the client is clear about what he or she is working toward and knows when the goal has been reached. For example, the goal of increasing social support might include starting a conversation with a new person each week, inviting a friend to a social activity each week, or calling a person the client met in a support group. Note that goals can also involve the expression of feelings. For example, a goal can be to talk about three feelings a day to foster parents. Sometimes the specifics of goals are delineated in objectives underneath that particular goal. For instance, a patient in a long-term care unit, who was dependent on a ventilator for his breathing, had, as a goal, to get out of bed two times per week. Objectives under this goal included initating a conversation with the nursing staff as to when he would like activity to take place; complying within 5 to 7 seconds with staff requests to move his arm or leg; and remaining out of bed and up in his wheelchair for a minimum of 3 hours before requesting to get back in bed. (See Chapter 3 for more on this case.)

11. *Determine the client's level of commitment to the goal.* Commitment or motivation to a certain goal can be determined quickly through the use of a scale: "From 1 to 10, with 1 being not at all important and 10 being very important, where would you place yourself?" Hepworth, Rooney, and Larsen (2002) recommend that clients at least be at a 7 in relation to wanting to achieve the goal; otherwise they may not be sufficiently motivated.

EXAMPLE 1–4

Shawnette is a 16-year-old African American female enrolled in the eleventh grade at a local high school. Shawnette has been part of a therapeutic foster care program for the past 2 years. She was placed because her mother had a severe mental illness, making her unable to manage Shawnette, and no other family members were available. Shawnette sometimes gets in trouble for arguing with adults, the other youths in her program, and her classmates. She is also failing three of her classes.

When the social work intern began talking with her, Shawnette said that out of all her concerns, she is most worried about her classes. "If I don't pass them, I'll never graduate from high school. I only have one year left after this one, and that doesn't leave me enough time to make up classes that I fail." To explain her grades, Shawnette admitted she doesn't do her homework and, in fact, never opens a book. She sleeps in class and has difficulty understanding chemistry and geometry, and so she has just given up. She said the reason she's failing English is that she simply chooses not to do the work—not because she does not understand it but because she thinks it's "stupid."

The social work intern introduced the idea of goals:

Social work intern: If you had to identify one goal that you would like to accomplish for yourself right now, what do you think it might be? It can be either a big goal or a small one.

Shawnette: I want to graduate from high school.

Social work intern: That's a really impressive goal. It's a large, long-term goal, so what we are going to do now is break it down into smaller steps that will have to be taken.

Shawnette: Well, I need to pass chemistry, English, and geometry.

Social work intern: Let's look at what goals we can set for each of those classes, since they're all so different and present different problems. Which one would you like to start with?

Shawnette: Chemistry. I've been doing the worst in that class. I don't understand anything. It's so hard, I just gave up trying.

Social work intern: I hear you're pretty frustrated with that class because it's so difficult for you. Chemistry can be difficult for many people. What ideas do you have about what can help you with chemistry?

Shawnette: Well, my teacher is always offering extra help if we stay after school, but I just haven't done it yet. I guess I could do that.

Social work intern: Tell me how you would approach your teacher and what you would say.

They went through a role play, which reduced the barrier of Shawnette's not knowing what to say or how to ask for help.

Another goal Shawnette identified for the week was to do her English homework at least once. This involved several tasks: writing down assignments, taking her books home, setting aside time to do her work, and finding a quiet place in the house to do this. Shawnette also said she would stay awake during her geometry class and listen to what was going on. In order to do this, Shawnette said she would bring a drink to class and engage in self-talk (e.g., "I am listening to what is going on").

In the next contact with the intern, Shawnette reported some success: she had scheduled and attended a meeting with her chemistry teacher. She also said she was able to do her English homework once, and her teacher complimented her for handing it in. Writing the homework down, taking her books home, and doing homework right after school helped her achieve this step.

Shawnette said that she stayed awake in geometry but became very frustrated because she did not understand any of the material. She didn't think she could catch up because she was so far behind. She came up with a couple of ideas on her own for the next week. She would ask for tutoring help from her geometry teacher. If that was not successful, Shawnette said she would talk with her school counselor and see what could be done.

Example 1–4 shows how the intern helped a client with a goal she had identified. The goal was partialized and broken down into constituent tasks that were manageable for the client to achieve.

Exercise 1-5

In the following scenarios, identify problems with the stated goals and suggest solutions.

1. A client suffering from depression says she just wants to feel happier.

2. A mother states her goal as "My family needs to communicate better."

3. An adolescent girl seen by a social work intern at a juvenile justice detention center says she doesn't have any goals for herself and doesn't want to work on any.

4. A man whose girlfriend broke up with him because of his physical violence says that his goal is "for her to take me back."

5. A parent whose 7-year-old child has been acting out at school (shooting spitballs, laughing and making loud jokes to the classroom at large, talking when the teacher is talking, not doing work) says that her goal is for the social worker to "talk some sense into him" and "make him see right." She admits that he is similarly disruptive at home.

6. A man who has been referred for substance abuse treatment says his goal is to quit drinking.

7. A seventh grader who is being seen by the school social work intern is currently not doing any homework (he usually gets three homework assignments per day). The school social work intern decides that his goal should be "to do all his homework."

8. A child protective services worker writes up her initial quarterly case plan. She decides the client's goals should be to (1) seek better housing, (2) attend a battered women's group, (3) participate in a parenting skills group, and (4) receive job skills training. For the client's child, who has been diagnosed with autism, the caseworker draws up some other goals that involve the mother: (1) seek services at a clinic that specializes in pervasive developmental disorders, (2) attend a support group related to her child's disability, and (3) take the child for individual therapy to develop attachment.

Exercise 1-6

Considering the guidelines for goals that have been set forth, think about an area in your life that you would like to change. Describe a possible goal for accomplishing this change.

Exercise 1-7

Considering the guidelines for goals that have been set forth, describe a possible goal for a client on your caseload (recognizing that you are leaving out an important guideline, which is to include client input).

The next section discusses ways in which the social worker can track goals and evaluate the outcome of the work. The focus is on scaling questions and single-system designs.

Evaluation

Scaling Questions

Scaling questions are a goal-setting intervention developed by solution-focused therapists in which clients rank-order themselves in relation to a goal (de Jong & Berg, 2001). They can be used not only as a clinical tool but also as a way to assess baseline behaviors, progress, and outcome. The following steps help the social worker utilize the scale effectively. Also see Chapter 4 for the use of this technique when working with client belief systems.

1. **Construct the scale.** Pictorially representing a scale with 10-point increments, describe to the client a scale of 1 to 10 with 10 as "when the problem you came here for is solved."

2. **Anchor at 10 what the client wants to achieve.** The goal should be phrased in terms of the presence of the positive ("feeling better") rather than as the absence of the negative ("not feeling depressed"). Ten should be realistic and achievable rather than "when everything is perfect." Get the client to identify at least three behavioral or cognitive indicators of what will be happening when the problem is solved. Sometimes clients can be helped to understand the idea of behavioral indicators by using the analogy of looking at them through a videoplayer ("If I were looking through a videoplayer, what would I see you doing?"). For instance, in a client who wants to feel better from depression, behavioral indicators might be "seeing friends once a week," "exercising twice a week," "finding a class to sign up for to get me out of the house," and thinking, "My life is going fine." Even when clients talk about nebulous goals or states, such as motivation, feeling happy, and increased self-esteem, they are then forced to put these goals into behavioral and cognitive terms by having to describe a picture of what 10 will look like.

The endpoint of the scale needs to be fleshed out thoroughly, since the assumption is that this will shift people's attention to a vision of what they want rather than what they don't want. There is no need to anchor each point of the 10 increments, however. Rank-ordering relies on clients' perceptions of where they are in terms of their problem being solved.

3. *Have the client rank-order him or herself on the scale.* The next part of the scaling intervention involves asking clients to rank-order themselves in relation to 10. Clients often place themselves at a number implying change has already occurred, which allows them to see that their problems are not as all-encompassing as previously believed. Occasionally, clients place themselves at a 1; in these cases, the social worker can inquire about times when the problem is "... less severe, frequent, intense or shorter in duration" (O'Hanlon & Weiner-Davis, 1989, p. 86) or what the client is doing to prevent problems from getting even worse.

The scales pose an advantage in terms of helping people get in touch with the strengths they have already demonstrated. For example, sometimes people initially discuss a problem at great length and become very negative about its all-pervasive nature. However, when they are asked to rank themselves, they give a number that is much higher than the initial discussion might indicate. The scale gives them a concrete reminder that they are moving toward solving their problem.

As was emphasized earlier, rank-ordering is based on the client's perception. Therefore, avoid challenging the client about the rating. One way to get at possible disparities in how others might view the client is through relationship questions.

4. *Ask relationship questions.* Relationship questions, questions about where others may perceive the client on the scale, are asked so that clients may gain a different perspective (de Jong & Berg, 2001). The social worker might ask, for example, "Where would your supervisor place you on the scale?" Clients who suffer from cognitive distortions often view themselves differently from how others experience them. Getting clients to perceive themselves from someone else's perspective may help them see themselves more realistically. With certain problems, such as depression, clients tend to see others as ranking them higher on their competence and hope for the future than they rank themselves. With other problems, such as juvenile offending, clients tend to view themselves as

doing better than what others may perceive. In either case, relationship questions challenge clients to appraise themselves more appropriately through the viewpoint of others.

5. *Set achievable tasks.* Task setting can also be formulated from the solution-focused scale. Clients are called upon to determine how they will move up one rank order (a 10 percent change) during the time between the next contact with the social worker. There is no need to embark on a more ambitious plan—to move from a 4 to a 10, for instance. Instead, a focus on a 10 percent change breaks down the problem and its commensurate solution into manageable units. Small changes that are easily achieved are more likely to spark further positive actions. If clients are able to adjust their behavior, they often feel better. They may also see a corresponding difference in the way others react to them. Consequently, they become more willing to take further steps toward their goals.

6. *Monitoring progress.* The solution-focused scale can be used in subsequent sessions in order to track progress over time and to determine when goals have been met. Tracking progress in this way makes attainment toward goals quantifiable and measurable.

Exercise 1-8

Considering the steps just described, construct a scale and follow the steps. Ideally, perform this exercise with an actual client with whom you are working. Otherwise, apply this exercise to a hypothetical situation or role play with another student posing as a client.

Single-Subject Designs

Single-subject designs (also called single-case and single-system designs) can be used to assess progress on a targeted behavior. Information for designing and implementing single-subject designs is drawn from Rubin and Babbie (2005). This section introduces the simplest single-subject design, the A-B design, and explains how to do visual analysis of the data points. We stop short of statistical analysis of the data points; information about statistical analysis of single-subject designs and more complex designs is available in Rubin and Babbie and other research texts.

The first step of designing a single-system study is to decide the behavior to be targeted based on your assessment of the client's problem and goal formulation. The next step is to decide who will collect the data. Behaviors can be tracked through different sources, including

- client self-report
- another person's report
- behavioral observation

Usually, adults can track their own thoughts and behaviors unless they are incapacitated in some way. However, another person's report might be more accurate for certain problems. For instance, in domestic violence, it is generally believed that the person who has been abused is a more accurate reporter of violence or threats of violence than is the person doing the abusing. For child problems, especially those involving externalizing behaviors, parents' and teachers' reports are considered more useful. Sometimes you, as the social worker, might conduct behavioral observations to assess the frequency of a behavior. For instance, in working with a child, you might track the number of times in a session the child followed your directions.

The next step in designing the single-subject design, and sometimes the most challenging, involves collecting baseline data. A baseline helps us to understand, given the occurrence of the problem before intervention, how intervention has helped change the problem. The general guidelines are to gather five to ten data points as a baseline and to stay within a month's timeframe. This can be done in one of two ways; intervention can be withheld until this information is collected, or the baseline can be constructed retrospectively.

In the types of problems social workers see, which are serious in nature and usually require immediate intervention, withholding intervention for a period of time might be detrimental to the client. An obvious problem with retrospective reporting, however, is that it can be biased due to the extent of people's ability to recall, especially when their memories are clouded by a present problem. For example, a person who is depressed typically remembers the recent past as depressing.

After the baseline data has been gathered, intervention begins and the same data is collected throughout the intervention period. The social worker plots the data points on a graph with the horizontal axis representing the time increments chosen for data observation (e.g., are the data points being measured twice daily, daily, weekly?). The vertical axis is the level of measurement chosen to assess the target behavior, such as the frequency in numbers, yes or no for whether or not the behavior occurred, or a Likert-type measurement (always, sometimes, hardly ever, never).

Clinically, the graph can be very useful; as the social worker discusses with the client the extent of progress, a client can be encouraged by the work he or she is doing by noting that improvement is being made. The social worker and client can also talk about other events that have occurred during intervention that might have impacted progress in particular ways. Alternatively, if the work is not progressing as planned, the social worker and client can discuss the possible reasons, and can revise the intervention plan as appropriate.

EXAMPLE 1–5

A social work intern at a battered women's shelter worked with Mimi, a Nigerian refugee. Mimi had left her husband because he was violent with her on many occasions during their marriage, both when they lived in Nigeria and after they came to the United States. The most recent episode occurred the night Mimi went to the shelter: her husband struck her face with his fist, causing a bruise. Prior to his hitting her, Mimi had questioned him about where he had been that night. She knew he was seeing another woman and thought that he had been with her.

The intern started working with Mimi the morning after she came to the shelter. At the first meeting, Mimi was very distraught and worried about what would become of her and her three children if she separated from her husband, since he was the family provider. At the same time, she no longer wanted to live with his violence, and his seeing another woman was intolerable.

After the intern explored Mimi's feelings, she asked Mimi about her thoughts. Mimi described her "worry" thoughts as the following: "How am I going to make it? I have no money and three children to take care of." "I don't deserve anyone better than him." "This is just what a woman has to put up with." "It's awful here at the shelter. Living back home would be better than this." "I'm not going to be able to afford a place of my own, and we're going to become homeless." "My children will starve to death." "I don't have the right to deprive them of their father." "He's right, I don't have any choice but to put up with this." "I'm not like these other women at the shelter. I don't belong here." "What are people I know going to say about what I'm doing?"

Mimi said that she had not been able to sleep at all the night before because of these thoughts. In order to collect a baseline, the intern asked Mimi to be aware of her thoughts and to give herself a check mark for each time she had a "worry" thought about leaving her husband.

The intern explained some of the dynamics of family violence and the laws and mores in this country about domestic violence, which Mimi then contrasted with those observed in Nigeria. The intern then explained the resources that were available to Mimi and what she could do to get some of them initiated, such as signing a complaint with the police, filing a protective order with the county attorney's office, and applying for emergency food stamps at the local benefits office. The intern also informed her of transitional housing that was available to battered women and their families so that they could start to build independent lives. Mimi said she was interested, so the intern scheduled an intake appointment for her at the battered women's outreach office.

As the intern drove her to these various resources (Mimi did not know how to drive), she could see that Mimi often looked upset and seemed to be ruminating quietly. The intern would ask Mimi about the thoughts running through her mind and prompt her to write them in the notebook she had given her.

Note that the intern started some intervention—educating Mimi about family violence and connecting her with resources—during the baseline period. Since Mimi's safety was endangered by the family violence and she had to be quickly engaged in services before she gave up and went back to her husband, it was critical that the intern inform her immediately of the community supports and resources available to her. In addition, the intern did not yet start the technique of cognitive restructuring, the intervention she was interested in monitoring for its impact on Mimi. Cognitive restructuring is a technique in which the social worker assesses the client's patterns of thinking and, through a series of discussions and exercises, helps the client dispute dysfunctional thoughts and beliefs and replace them with more functional patterns. (See Chapter 4 for complete information on cognitive restructuring.)

The following week, Mimi provided the baseline data she had collected over the course of the week. Figure 1-3 shows that Mimi had a high number of worry thoughts each day, never fewer than 475. At this point, the intern taught Mimi the technique of cognitive restructuring so that she could begin to challenge some of her worry thoughts and replace them with more realistic and positive thinking. She again instructed Mimi to keep tracking her worry thoughts each day, but this time she was also to use cognitive restructuring to counteract these thoughts.

During that day and the next, the intern continued to spend time with Mimi, taking her to register for welfare benefits and to the county attorney's office to file a protective order. She prompted

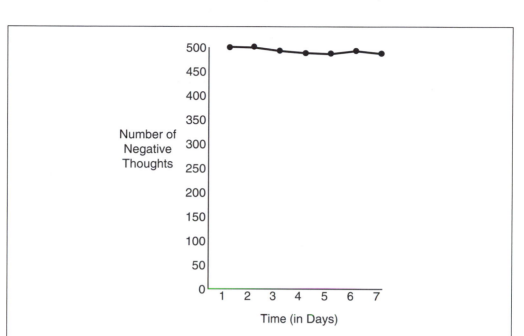

Figure 1–3 Mimi's baseline of negative thoughts.

Mimi about her thoughts and helped Mimi challenge some of the worry thoughts and replace them with more positive thinking. As the intern would not be in the office until the following week, she instructed Mimi to continue recording and challenging thoughts. The intern informed staff at the shelter about the work Mimi was doing so that they could continue to work with her on it.

When the intern returned the following week, she went over with Mimi the results of her "homework." Mimi had diligently recorded her worry thoughts and had also applied the process of cognitive restructuring. By the next day when they again met, the intern had gathered all the baseline and intervention data collected so far and had plotted the information on a graph (Figure 1-4). Mimi could see that although the number of worry thoughts was still very high, it was gradually decreasing.

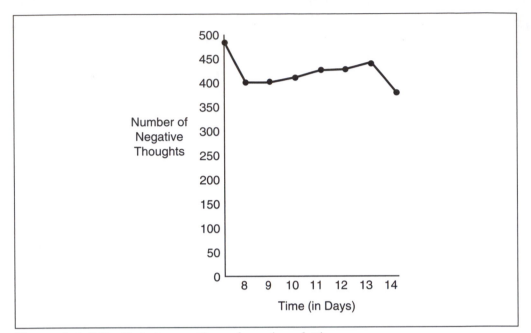

Figure 1–4 Mimi's intervention phase (week 1).

The intern continued to work with Mimi on this technique and on connecting her with resources. The work ended when Mimi left the shelter after the maximum time limit of 3 weeks. Figure 1–5 shows the completed single-subject design for Mimi. When they reviewed the data during their final meeting, Mimi realized that she had made progress, as her worry thoughts continued to decrease. She said that the technique of cognitive restructuring had been helpful for her and she would continue to use it as she and her children moved into transitional living arrangements.

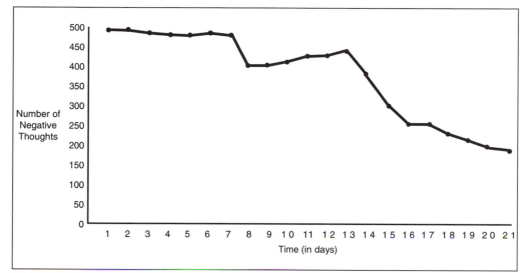

Figure 1–5 Mimi's single-subject design.

Exercise 1-9

Considering the steps described and the example provided, construct a single-subject design. Ideally, perform this exercise with an actual client with whom you are working. Otherwise, apply this exercise to a hypothetical situation or role play with another student posing as a client.

Summary

Cognitive-behavioral approaches are highly oriented toward defining problems in terms of behavioral specifics and measurable goals. Such approaches emphasize evaluation of client progress. Increasingly, the social worker will find it necessary to show accountability in practice. In line with this focus, this chapter covered behavioral assessment, goal setting, and ways to track client progress on goals over time.

References

Azar, S. T., & Wolfe, D. A. (1998). Child abuse and neglect. In E. J. Mash & R. A. Barkley (Eds.), *Treatment of childhood disorders*, 2nd ed. (pp. 501–544). New York: Guilford Press.

Berg, I. K., & Miller, S. (1992). *Working with the problem drinker*. New York: W.W. Norton.

Bertolino, B., & O'Hanlon, B. (2002). *Collaborative, competency-based counseling and therapy*. Boston: Allyn & Bacon.

Brestan, E., & Eyberg, S. (1998). Effective psychological treatments of conduct-disordered children and adolescents: 29 years, 82 studies, and 5,272 kids. *Journal of Clinical Child Psychology, 27*, 180–189.

Cade, B., & O'Hanlon, W. H. (1993). *A brief guide to brief therapy*. New York: W.W. Norton.

Carroll, K. (1998). *A cognitive-behavioral approach: Treating cocaine addiction*. Online: http://www.drugabuse.gov/TXManuals/CBT/CBT1.html. Accessed August 28, 2004.

Christensen, D., Todahl, J., & Barrett, W. (1999). *Solution-based casework: An introduction to clinical and case management skills in casework practice*. New York: Aldine De Gruyter.

De Jong, P., & Berg, I. K. (2001). *Interviewing for solutions*, 2nd ed. Pacific Grove, CA: Brooks/Cole.

Hepworth, D. H., Rooney, R., & Larsen, J. (2002). *Direct social work practice: Theory & skills*, 6th ed. Belmont, CA: Brooks/Cole.

O'Hanlon, W. H., & Weiner-Davis, M. (1989). *In search of solutions: A new direction in psychotherapy*. New York: W.W. Norton.

Rubin, A. & Babbie, E. (2005). *Research methods for social work*, 5th ed. Belmont, CA: Brooks-Cole.

Serketich, W. J., & Dumas, J. E. (1996). The effectiveness of behavioral parent training to modify antisocial behavior in children: A meta-analysis. *Behavior Therapy, 27*, 171–186.

2

— ▼▲▼ —

Behavioral Interventions

Behaviorism has been prominent in the social sciences since the first half of the twentieth century, and it became a popular theory among clinical practitioners in the 1960s. Among its pioneers were Pavlov (1932, 1934), Watson (1930), and Skinner (1953). The rise of behaviorism reflected the new emphasis in the social sciences on empiricism (observable evidence) in evaluating the outcomes of clinical intervention.

This chapter covers some of the basic principles and methods of behavior theory. All behavior is influenced by the same principles of learning, which include classical conditioning, operant conditioning, and modeling. Examples and exercises to familiarize you with these concepts are interspersed throughout the chapter. We focus on techniques from a branch of behaviorism called *operant conditioning* because they have the broadest practice applications.

Classical Conditioning

Conditioning is a process of developing patterns of behavior through responses to environmental stimuli or specific behavioral consequences (Wilson, 2000). The earliest behavioral research involved classical conditioning in which an initially neutral stimulus comes to produce a conditioned response after being paired repeatedly with a conditioned stimulus (Pavlov, 1932, 1934). In Pavlov's famous research, food (the conditioned stimulus) naturally produced salivation (a nonvoluntary response) in dogs. A bell (the unconditioned stimulus) initially failed to evoke salivation. However, after the bell was paired with the food, over time, the dogs started to salivate when presented with the bell alone. The bell at this point attained the status of a conditioned stimulus, since it was capable of producing a response.

Classical conditioning plays a role in the understanding of many behavioral problems that clients experience (Gambrill, 1994). For example, previously neutral cues, such as certain places (restaurants or bars), people, or feeling states (e.g., boredom) may become associated with problem behaviors such as overeating or substance abuse. Many anxiety-related disorders are also classically conditioned. For instance, a bad experience giving a presentation in a group might generalize to a fear of all public presentations.

During clinical intervention, the principles of classical conditioning are reversed. For example, if a client experiences an urge to use drugs when experiencing a particular emotion, such as boredom, the conditional pairing between boredom and drug use could eventually lose its association if the person abstained from using drugs to counteract boredom over a period of time. The urge to use drugs is thus extinguished.

Classical conditioning is also involved with the treatment of anxiety. Fear-laden cues, such as those associated with a sexual assault, are rank-ordered by the client and social worker according to the level of fear they invoke. Clients learn to face each event or item on the list, starting with the least anxiety provoking, by learning to pair relaxation exercises and other coping strategies with the event rather than associating it with anxiety. Relaxation processes might include deep breathing, deep muscle relaxation, and visualization. In this process of systematic desensitization (Wolpe, 1958), people work their way through the rank ordering of fears until they are no longer plagued by the anxiety.

Operant Conditioning

The main premise of operant conditioning is that future behavior is determined by the consequences of present behavior (Skinner, 1953). Two types of reinforcement are discussed: positive and negative. Both encourage certain behaviors to occur in the future. *Positive* reinforcement increases the behavior preceding it. For instance, alcohol use is positively reinforced by the resultant feelings of well-being and pleasant social interaction with others. In other words, a person learns that drinking may lead to some pleasurable conse-quences; he or she may be susceptible to using alcohol in the future to produce these positive results.

Through *negative* reinforcement, a person's behavior leads him or her to avoid, escape from, or stop an unpleasant event, making the behavior more likely to occur in the future. Alcohol use, for example, is negatively reinforcing if it leads to escape from uncomfortable or distressing feelings (Carroll, 1998).

Most people find negative reinforcement a more difficult a concept to grasp than positive reinforcement. However, it is important to recognize when it occurs so that unhelpful reinforcement patterns can be broken.

Reinforcement patterns are often *reciprocal*; that is, one person in an inter-action may be positively reinforced by the other person, who in turn is nega-tively reinforced by the other. For instance, a common parent–child situation is one in which a child tantrums to receive what she wants (let's say, candy in a grocery store). If the parent gives candy to stop the tantrum, the child is being *positively reinforced* for tantrumming. At the same time, the parent is being neg-atively reinforced for giving in. By providing candy, the parent has stopped the aversive behavior (tantrumming). The parent learns that tantrums can be stopped by giving in. Unfortuately, the child simultaneously learns that she can get what she wants by tantrumming.

The following exercises will familiarize you further with the concepts of reinforcement.

Exercise 2-1

In the following examples, indicate where positive and negative reinforcement is taking place and explain which behaviors are being reinforced.

1. A child makes distracting noises while a teacher is talking until the teacher reprimands him. He stops after the teacher reprimands him,

but he keeps making a nuisance of himself in class. Consider reinforcement from the perspective of both the adult and the child.

2. A woman with anxiety about public speaking calls in sick the day she has to present in front of a group.

3. An instructor praises a student for asking a question in class.

4. A woman in a violent relationship leaves her partner. However, she misses him and feels very alone. She returns to him, and they both feel intensely happy.

5. Playing off the same scenario in 4, the woman's partner treats her well when she returns.

6. A 2½-year-old child with autism refuses to eat many foods. His parents therefore give him only food he enjoys, such as pudding and cookies.

7. A child, when he puts away his toys, is told by his father that he is doing a good job.

8. A mother attends a parenting class, and the social worker leading the class praises her for coming each week.

Exercise 2-2

Think of examples from your own life in which positive and negative reinforcement take place and record them here.

Positive reinforcement:

Negative reinforcement:

Now that you are more familiar with reinforcement principles, we turn to practice interventions. You may already know about the behavioral methods that are taught to parents to gain control of their children's behaviors. These methods are called *parent training* in which parents are taught to reinforce their children's prosocial behaviors and extinguish negative behaviors through ignoring them or using punishments (Patterson, 1971). However, the same techniques can be used in any setting in which people assume environmental control over the behaviors of others. The remainder of this chapter details the types of reinforcement that can be applied in practice situations. Also discussed is how to make effective commands and requests. Finally, the techniques of extinction and punishment are covered.

Reinforcement

Types of reinforcement involve social reinforcement, the use of high-probability behaviors, and token economies. It is commonly believed among behaviorists that reinforcement is more effective than punishment. At least for children, it is suggested that only after a new behavior has been reinforced for a week should punishment for the opposite, undesired behavior be initiated (Barkley, 2000). Even then, positive reinforcement should outweigh punishment by about three to one.

You should also be familiar with the *schedule of reinforcement*—that is, how often reinforcement is applied after the desired behavior has been performed. Continuous reinforcement is when reinforcement is supplied after each instance of the desired behavior. Intermittent reinforcement is when reinforcement is provided irregularly. The general guideline is to reinforce a behavior every time it occurs until it is in place; after that time, intermittent reinforcement is sufficient to maintain the behavior. You may already know that intermittent reinforcement is the strongest schedule of reinforcement. Note the popularity of slot machines, for instance!

SOCIAL REINFORCEMENT

Social reinforcement is our initial focus because it is the easiest to apply and is already within most people's repertoire. In addition, other reinforcement systems typically incorporate social reinforcement as well. Social reinforcement involves praise, smiles, winks, thumbs-up signs, hugs, pats on the head or shoulder, and so on. The guidelines for praise, a major form of social reinforcement, include the following (Webster-Stratton, 2001):

- praising immediately after the behavior is performed instead of waiting to do it later
- praising effort and progress rather than just achievement or perfection
- labeling praise (describing specifically what the person has done to deserve praise so they know what behaviors to repeat) rather than making global statements, such as "What a good boy!"
- coupling verbal praise with eye contact, a smile, and/or physical affection
- avoid accompanying praise with criticism ("You did a good job washing the dishes, but why can't you dry them right?")
- avoid arguing about the praise and ignore inappropriate responses instead (the person being praised says, "I did not do a good job. Why are you lying to me?")

Exercise 2–3

Select a behavior you would like to see increase in a person in your life. This person could be a client, a child, a romantic partner, a friend, a roommate, a fellow classmate, or an instructor. Write down the behavior. Praise that behavior every time it occurs for the following week and report the results here.

HIGH-PROBABILITY BEHAVIORS

High-probability behaviors are another type of reinforcement system (Kazdin, 2001). They involve the activities that people automatically engage in for pleasure and relaxation, such as playing outside, talking on the phone, using the Internet, playing video games, and watching TV. To use these activities as reinforcement, they have to be withheld until the person has performed a certain task or behavior first. An advantage of using high-probability behaviors as reinforcement is that it relies on behaviors that are already present; one does not need to set up a new system of reinforcement.

Exercise 2–4

Try a system of a high-probability behavior as reinforcement for yourself. Select a pleasurable activity that you already do on a regular basis. Now pick a chore or a task that you find less compelling (schoolwork, for instance). For one day, do that high-probability behavior only after you complete the chore or task. Write down the activity and task here and report your results the day after you do this assignment.

TOKEN ECONOMIES

Another type of reinforcement system involves token economies in which points or tokens (stickers, stars, checks, coins) are given for desirable behaviors and are then traded in for an agreed-upon reward (Barkley, 2000). You might already be familiar with token economies from your social work setting. In a residential placement or a treatment facility, certain privileges, such as weekends home, more time alone, and field trips, are often contingent upon earning points or reaching "levels" by displaying certain desired behaviors.

Token economies have a number of advantages. They can bridge the gap between the desired behavior and the reward (Kazdin, 2001). They are a tangible reminder to individuals that they are getting closer to earning their reward. Points can be attached to different tasks that may comprise a desired goal when the behavior involved is complex. For instance, "getting to school on time" may comprise several behavioral sequences (getting out of bed, bathing, eating breakfast, getting dressed, and making sure all supplies are together). Each part in the sequence can be reinforced rather than waiting until the whole behavior is performed. Further, tokens can be quickly and easily administered without interrupting the desired behavior. In addition, tokens are less prone to satiation. When agreed-upon rewards lose their reinforcing value, they can simply be exchanged for other rewards (Kazdin, 2001). Although we are talking about token economies in the context of reinforcement, they can be used for punishment as well. For instance, points can be withdrawn for offensive behaviors.

EXAMPLE 2–1

Table 2–1 represents a token economy chart for, Miguel, a 10-year-old Hispanic boy whose parents complained that he does not complete his homework and chores and that he argues instead of following directions. You can see in this example that Miguel receives a check mark for each day of the week he performs certain desired behaviors. Miguel is responsible for the following chores: clearing common living spaces of toys, games, schoolwork, shoes, and other personal items; taking out the garbage; and doing dishes. He also typically has three homework assignments a day; these are delineated separately. Each day, Miguel's parents must know whether homework is indeed assigned in each of these classes and if homework assignments from other classes are added. In other words, the parents must know the total number of homework assignments for that week in order to compute the number Miguel earned out of that total. It must also be determined in advance what number of checks marks will yield Miguel a certain reward.

TABLE 2–1 **Sample Token Economy Chart: Miguel**

Behavior	M	T	W	Th	F	S	Sun	Points
Doing dishes after dinner								
Taking garbage out								
Doing math homework assignment								
Doing social studies homework assignment								
Doing English homework assignment								
Following instructions without arguing								
Points								Total

Other complexities exist even in this very basic example. For instance, Miguel might not have to take the garbage out every night—perhaps only twice a week when the garbage is collected. For the behavior of "following instructions without arguing," there are probably many opportunities for this behavior throughout a particular day. For instance, on the first day of the token economy, Miguel's parents talk it over and find that, between them, Miguel argued on four occasions and didn't follow instructions; three times he didn't argue, although he also did not follow instructions; and two times he completed what they had asked of him. Miguel's parents, for that day, decided to withhold a check mark for "following instructions."

As you can see from this example, the creation of effective token economies can be quite challenging, and a lot of thought must go into their construction. You will also note that, depending on the child's baseline behaviors, each behavior might lend itself to more detailed tasks that deserve their own tokens for completion. Let's say that Miguel is not doing any homework and his parents want to focus on this goal exclusively. Doing a particular homework assignment might involve (1) getting books and materials ready, (2) reading directions, (3) doing the assignment, (4) checking with a parent that the work has been done correctly, and (5) correcting the work.

Although token economies can be very useful, one drawback is that people have to be organized about implementing them consistently. Families that are already overwhelmed by multiple stressors may have some difficulty following through with the necessary structure. Some adaptations may be necessary so that parents experience a greater likelihood of success. First, the number of target behaviors identified on a token economy chart should be kept to an absolute minimum (perhaps three at the most). Second, the target behaviors should be the same for all children in a household in which there are multiple children. Third, the token economy chart should be kept in a high-traffic area, such as on the refrigerator, so that family members are frequently reminded of the system. Fourth, if it is possible, have parents allow the children to place the check marks (stickers, stars, etc.) on the chart themselves. This process is reinforcing in itself, and this way, children can take more ownership over their behavior.

Exercise 2-5

For this exercise, you are offered alternatives (A or B) depending on your type of field or work setting.

Choice A: If you are in a setting that uses a token economy of some kind, describe the system in place. Detail the behaviors that are reinforced and how they are reinforced.

How many tokens do people have to earn to gain rewards? What are the rewards?

Have you identified any problems with the token system, in either its setup or its implementation? What improvements would you make?

Choice B: If you are not working in a setting that uses a token economy system, consider how you would set one up in your internship or practice setting, either at the program level or with an individual client. What would you need to take into account to ensure that the token economy is effective?

Rewards

The terms *reinforcement* and *reward* are often used interchangeably but are actually different concepts. Reinforcement, by definition, increases the behavior that precedes it, whereas a reward is something given in return for a service or achievement and may or may not increase the frequency of a behavior (Kazdin, 2001). A common example that illustrates the difference involves a paycheck versus sales' incentives. A paycheck does not necessarily increase "work behavior" (i.e., it doesn't affect the amount of work you do). However, if you are given a monetary incentive for certain quotas of sales, then you may be motivated to work harder in order to get the incentive. Rewards, as was covered in the section on token economies, are sometimes given in exchange for a certain number of tokens earned.

When parents hear the word rewards, they often say they do not have enough money for rewards. Indeed, a good guideline to follow is that rewards should rely as much as possible on relationship factors (Hepworth, Rooney, & Larsen, 2002). For instance, time with a caregiver at the park, playing a game, or catching a ball can be very rewarding activities for children and can teach them the value of relationships rather than material objects.

EXAMPLE 2-2

Sonya, who was first introduced in Chapter 1, Example 1–1, is the mother of three children and was having trouble managing 8-year-old Ellie's behavior.

Sonya talked about her use of rewards with Ellie:

Sonya: Last summer, Ellie's mentor wanted to take her to Six Flags, so I told her she could go if she did her chores every day for two weeks.

Intern: How did that work?

Sonya: Ellie didn't do *any* chores until the night before, and then she cleaned all night so she could go. I wasn't going to let her, but her mentor had already bought the tickets, so I didn't want to say no.

Exercise 2-6

What were some of the problems with how the reward was managed in this case? How could you more effectively implement the reward system?

After the social work intern had done more work with Sonya on the use of rewards, Sonya reported the following incident:

Sonya: I tried it. It didn't work. I told the kids that if they did their chores for a week, they could go over to their aunt's house. The kids *love* this woman. She goes to their church and their stepdad used to take them up to her house all the time over the summer. But *none* of them did their chores, and then come Sunday, they were all upset that I wouldn't let them go over there. But I was like, "I *told* you, you weren't going unless you did your chores. Did you do them? No!"

Exercise 2-7

How would you respond to Sonya in this situation?

Social service agencies sometimes have access to donated pleasure items, money for meals at fast-food restaurants, furniture, and so on. Clients often receive these "rewards" unconditionally; the items are simply given to clients because they are available. However, one way to use these items is as incentives for achievement of a particular behavior that has been clearly stated up front.

EXAMPLE 2-3

This example involves a social work intern at a homeless agency, where she worked with Daryl, a 27-year-old African American. He was shot 4 years ago and is now paralyzed on one side of his body. Although he cannot talk, he can partially hear and read lips. He can scribble messages, but has difficulty retrieving the correct words and spelling them. While community resources and services were available to him, Daryl had difficulty following through with his appointments, especially those involving a communication specialist for the disabled. The goal therefore became to increase the number of appointments he attended. The intern asked the client what would be reinforcing for him to receive for attending his appointments. They mutually agreed that he would get bus tickets, which were accessible to caseworkers at the agency.

After 2 weeks of the behavioral system being implemented, the client had radically increased his appointment attendance. The caseworker planned to keep the system in place for the remainder of the semester. As he used the resources available to him, the ultimate goal was for Daryl's livelihood to improve. (Note that this case is also discussed in Chapter 8 in terms of overcoming some of the barriers that arose.)

Exercise 2-8

What is your reaction to the use of bus tickets as rewards for Daryl's attendance at community referral appointments? This might work well as a topic of class discussion, because there is no "right" answer.

Exercise 2-9

In your setting are there items or activities that are routinely provided to clients but that could be used as rewards instead? Describe them and the behaviors that could be rewarded. What must you do to make sure that the rewards work in the way you intend?

Commands and Requests

Although operant conditioning relies primarily on reinforcement contingencies, attention is also paid to stimulus conditions (events that are in place before the target behavior). Commands are one such part of the stimulus that make certain behaviors more likely to happen. The general guidelines outlined in this section can be applied to adults as well as to children, although adults are usually not given "commands"; rather they are "requested" to carry out certain behaviors.

The first guideline is to model appropriate behavior by being polite rather than yelling when issuing commands. A second guideline is to use only commands that are necessary rather than giving too many. Imagine you are performing a role play of an interview situation. If the instructor gave you suggestions every time you said something, what would be the effect on you? If you're like most people, you would feel stifled and anxious. Too many commands also lead to negative interactions or to commands being ignored

(Webster-Stratton, 2001). Especially for young children, only one command at a time should be issued (e.g., "Make your bed" rather than "Make your bed, pick up your toys, and then pick up the clothes in the bathroom and put them in the hamper"). However, this is also a good principle to use with adults, particularly when they are in novel learning situations.

Being specific and clear is another guideline to making commands. In the role-play example, it would be much easier for you to respond to "make a statement reflecting the client's feelings" rather than "show empathy." In general, it is also better to phrase commands in terms of what should be done rather than what should not be done. For instance, which statement is more clear and positive: if the instructor says, "Don't go on too long," or "Wrap up the interview within one minute"? For both children and adults being brief rather than lecturing is a good rule of thumb. Many children, for instance, lose the gist of their parent's message once that parent has gone on for too long and been repetitive or tangential to the matter at hand.

Some children (and even grown-ups!) are adept at arguing when they are asked to carry out a behavior. Such arguments should be avoided. The reason for giving a particular command or request should be brief, to the point, and not given more than once (Webster-Stratton, 2001).

A person's compliance with a command represents an opportunity to praise. As a result, a person often feels good about performing the behavior, knows he or she is on the right track, and may feel more positively toward you. The result is that he or she may be more likely to listen to you in the future.

Exercise 2-10

Center on an interaction in you life in which you have had some difficulty getting a person to follow through with an activity that you want him or her to do. Considering the guidelines in this section, construct an appropriate command or request of that person and then make the request. Record the reaction you received to your request. Did you get what you wanted? If not, discuss some of the possible reasons and how these might be addressed.

Extinction

In behavioral terms, *extinction* (also called *ignoring*) involves the process of no longer reinforcing a behavior, resulting in a decrease in the behavior or its possible eradication (Kazdin, 2001). For example, if a child's throwing tantrums in stores has gotten her what she wants (candy), ignoring the behavior eventually breaks the connection between the tantrum and getting candy.

For ignoring to work, you have to understand what has been reinforcing the person's undesirable behavior (Kazdin, 2001). An example involves a child misbehaving in school. Is the child misbehaving because he gets sent to the principal's office (gets out of class), or is he misbehaving so that he gets the teacher's attention? In the former case, extinction would involve not allowing the child to leave the class no matter how obnoxious his behavior becomes. In the latter case, extinction involves withdrawing attention from the child when he misbehaves.

Ignoring should be reserved for behaviors that are annoying rather than those that present a risk for injury. For instance, if a child is playing with household objects that may cause injury, ignoring is not the technique of choice; more direct action needs to be taken to ensure the child's safety.

Ignoring means avoiding eye contact with and not talking to the person whose behavior you're trying to make extinct. It might even involve leaving the room. For instance, if a child whines to get out of doing homework, a parent may have to leave the room so that ignoring can be successful. Of course, this might not be feasible in some situations. A teacher can't leave a classroom to ignore a child.

One important point to stress if you are enacting this technique or you are teaching it to someone else is that ignoring works *in a gradual way*. Although there are some lucky instances when results are immediate, generally, people who are being ignored keep at the behavior for awhile because it has worked so well for them in the past. That is the powerful nature of reinforcement at work.

For the technique to be successful, one must understand the concept of an "extinction burst." Expecting to elicit the reinforcement that used to work, a person might redouble his efforts to obtain it. As this occurs, it becomes extremely uncomfortable for the person to continue ignoring in the face of escalating behavior (for instance, a child whose whining behavior is being extinguished might now cry, scream, and throw a tantrum). The positive aspect to an extinction burst is that it signals that the extinction process is working—the "dark before the dawn." Of course, ignoring should also be accompanied by positive reinforcement for appropriate behaviors (Kazdin, 2001).

Exercise 2-11

In the following scenarios, name the particular technique that is being used. Identify the problems, if any, in the application of techniques.

1. To get their children (4- and 6-year-old girls) to stay in bed all night instead of coming into their parents' room three times a night, the parents decided to use a sticker system. A daily sticker would be given to each girl for staying in her bed all night and a prize would be awarded at the end of the week for the girl who stayed in her bed every night.

2. A woman who has left her violent boyfriend is now receiving phone messages from him. With each successive call, his messages become more intense. First he wonders where she is, then he is angry, then he tells her that he misses her and wants her back, and then he says he can't live without her. Finally, afraid that he is suicidal, she calls him back.

3. A social work student works with a mother of two boys, ages 10 and 8. The mother is worried about her sons' fighting with each other. The student teaches the mother about extinction. The mother says she will use ignoring unless it looks like her younger son is really going to get hurt.

Punishment

Punishment involves providing adverse consequences (e.g., physical discipline, harsh words, criticism) or the removal of positive events (e.g., privileges, points, time out from reinforcement) for the negative target behavior. The result is that the behavior decreases (Kazdin, 2001). Other punishments involve those based on effort or work (e.g., extra chores), restraining (only to be used when the child is a danger to self or others), and overcorrection. Since *overcorrection* is a form of punishment that is not as commonly used as some of the others, more detailed instruction on this technique is provided.

Overcorrection is a procedure in which the individual is required to correct the environmental effects of his or her inappropriate behavior (restitution) and then repeatedly practice appropriate forms of behavior (overcorrection) (Kazdin, 2001). An example of overcorrection involves a teenager who spray-paints on a building. Restitution involves the teen having to clean the spray paint off of the building. Positive practice involves the teen having to clean off several other spray-painted buildings as well.

The difference between punishment and negative reinforcement should be noted. Negative reinforcement results in the increase in behavior, while punishment has the effect of decreasing the frequency of a behavior. Some guidelines for punishment are provided, although it must be emphasized that using positive reinforcement, at least initially, is more effective than resorting right away to punishment. In addition, punishment is more effective when it is supplemented by positive reinforcement for the desired behavior. With these caveats in mind, the guidelines include the following (Kazdin, 2001):

> Punish the behavior every time it occurs until the behavior occurs only at low levels; then it is acceptable to punish intermittently.
>
> Increased intensity of punishment does not translate into more learning.
>
> Punishments should be ones that parents can maintain. (For instance, working parents often "ground" a teenager as punishment, even though they are not home in the afternoons to enforce this.)
>
> Verbal punishments, if used frequently, tend to lose their impact over time if they are not accompanied by other consequences.
>
> Immediate consequences are more effective than long-term consequences. For example, a child is repeatedly warned throughout the semester about the consequences of receiving a D on a class grade, which is that he can't play league ball during the summer. This will not have as much influence on his behavior as if he is punished more immediately for each poor grade he brings home on various assignments. First, his cognitive abilities make it difficult to bridge the time period of a whole semester. Second, parents may not have followed through before with consequences, so he may not be too concerned. Third, he might have performed some positive behaviors during the semester (perhaps on some assignments he did well); if he receives the D grade at the end of the semester, these positive behaviors may be inadvertently punished as well.

Also included here are some guidelines specific to time-out, since many people seem to have misperceptions about the procedures involved with this technique:

- The place for time-out should be free from reinforcement, meaning there should be no activities available, and the child is to do nothing.

- The time-out should be structured around a certain timeframe, generally one minute per year of the child's age.
- A child who attempts to engage others while he or she is in time-out should be ignored.
- If the child's behavior escalates into disruption, the time-out period resumes only after the child has gotten the behavior under control.
- After the time-out period is over, the child is to recount the reason for the punishment and what he or she has learned to do differently next time.

Many parents with whom social workers come in contact use physical discipline, and it is often difficult for parents to give up their belief that physical punishment represents effective discipline. Because this can be a potentially thorny issue, it is discussed at length in Chapter 8.

Exercise 2-12

In the following scenarios, describe what is problematic about the punishment and suggest a more effective form of punishment.

1. A stepfather of two boys, ages 7 and 8, describes his use of time-out as "putting them behind the sofa in the living room for two hours."

2. A 2-year-old's time-out comprises going to his room for 2 minutes. His room contains his toys and possesses a lot of visual stimulation (bright colors, pictures on the wall).

3. A mother whips her child with an extension cord because she "really needed to teach him a lesson."

4. An overstressed mother talks about how she yells at her children all the time, and they won't listen.

5. A teen is grounded for a report from school stating that he is failing three classes. His parents say that he can't go anywhere after school for the rest of the 6-week grading period (there are 2½ weeks remaining). Both parents work outside the home and don't return until 6:00 each night.

Exercise 2–13

1. Describe a recent example of how you used punishment in your everyday life.

2. Was it effective?

3. From what you have learned, can you now administer the punishment more effectively, or is there another form of punishment you can use?

4. Are you simultaneously using positive reinforcement? If you are not, how can you introduce positive reinforcement, either as a substitute for punishment or by employing it in addition to punishment?

Modeling and Behavior Rehearsal

Another way people learn behaviors is by watching others engage in them and being reinforced for them (Bandura, 1977). For instance, people may begin using alcohol or acting aggressively because they have seen their parents and other relatives acting this way. Modeling is one of the chief methods of behavioral change in cognitive-behavioral therapy. By modeling, the social worker shows the client how to enact a new behavior. The client then practices the new behavior (called behavioral rehearsal), receiving supportive feedback and suggestions for its refinement.

Covert modeling can also be used for intervention purposes. In covert rehearsal, the social worker guides the client through a process of imagining the completion of steps toward a successful outcome related to a goal. For example, an anxious client who must give a formal presentation may imagine herself approaching the public-speaking situation with ease and with the expectation that she will do well. She visualizes and feels herself speaking in a confident and calm manner and receiving a warm reception from the audience. The social worker "walks" the client through this process, and then the client rehearses it prior to the actual event.

The following steps are taken when modeling and behavioral rehearsal are used as change strategies (Hepworth et al., 2002):

1. *Social worker* **models** *skills.* The social worker demonstrates the skill so that the client can experience what it looks like. In this way, pressure is reduced on the client because he or she is not expected to perform a new behavior before it is modeled. At the same time, the social worker gains a fuller appreciation of the challenges the client faces. Sometimes, taking on the perspective of another person (such as family member, boss, friend) allows the client to more easily understand the other person's position. The process of taking on new roles also introduces a note of playfulness and humor to a situation that may have been previously viewed with grim seriousness.

2. *The social worker leads a discussion around the modeling that has occurred.* The social worker can share the difficulties he or she experienced in the process so that the client receives validation for the problem. The client can thus learn

that a "coping model" as opposed to a "mastery model" is adequate to get new interaction patterns going (Hepworth et al., 2002). The client can verbalize what was different as a result of the new interaction pattern. The social worker can clarify any elements of the skill that were still unclear and bolster confidence in the client to practice the new behavior.

3. *The client* **behaviorally rehearses** *the new skill.* The client practices the new behavior, which enables parts of the skill that were unclear or that were misunderstood to come to light for clarification. When the client experiences a different interaction pattern, it enhances his or her confidence that the skill can be generalized to a real-life situation.

4. *The client and social worker process the* **behavioral rehearsal.** The client expresses what it was like to try the new behavior and discusses what was different. The social worker offers compliments on areas that went well and feedback for improvement, if necessary. The client and social worker discuss potential barriers and challenges and how to circumvent these barriers. The client may be offered another opportunity to behaviorally rehearse if it seems necessary.

Detail on the modeling and behavioral rehearsal process is provided to emphasize that cognitive-behavioral therapy is helping clients learn new skills and learn to generalize these skills outside of the helping relationship to the real world. Many of the exercises in this workbook also ask you, if you do not have clients that are appropriate for certain applications, to role play with another student.

Exercise 2-14

Consider one of your behaviors that you believe you learned primarily from modeling. What is the behavior, and from whom did you learn it?

Exercise 2-15

Think of a client behavior and how modeling played a role in its learning. Write down the behavior and from whom the client learned it.

Summary

All situations in which people find themselves (except for truly novel ones), "cue" or prompt behaviors based on principles of classical conditioning (paired associations with certain aspects of the setting), operant conditioning (prior experiences in similar situations), or modeling (watching others behave). We focused primarily in this chapter on operant conditioning because it has a wide range of practice applications. Now that techniques have been detailed and you have had some experience with them by working through the exercises, the next chapter provides some lengthier case examples, showing how techniques can be put together.

References

Bandura, A. (1977). *Social learning theory.* Englewood Cliffs, NJ: Prentice-Hall.

Barkley, R. A. (2000). *Taking charge of ADHD*, rev. ed. New York: Guilford Press.

Carroll, K. (1998). *A cognitive-behavioral approach: Treating cocaine addiction.* Online: http://www.drugabuse.gov/TXManuals/CBT/CBT1.html. Accessed August 28, 2004.

Gambrill, E. D. (1994). Concepts and methods of behavioral treatment. In D. K. Granvold (Ed.), *Cognitive and behavioral treatment: Methods and applications* (pp. 32–62). New York: W.W. Norton & Company, Inc.

Hepworth, D. H., Rooney, R., & Larsen, J. (2002). *Direct social work practice: Theory & skills*, 6th ed. Belmont, CA: Brooks/Cole.

Kazdin, A. (2001). *Behavior modification in applied settings*, 6th ed. Pacific Grove, CA: Brooks/Cole.

Patterson, G. R. (1971). *Families: Application of social learning theory to family life.* Champaign, IL: Research Press.

Pavlov, I. P. (1932). Neuroses in man and animals. *Journal of The American Medical Association. 9*, 1012–1013.

Pavlov, I. P. (1934). An attempt at a physiological interpretation of obsessional neurosis and paranoia. *Journal of Mental Science, 80*, 187–197.

Skinner, B. F. (1953). *Science and human behavior.* New York: Macmillan.

Watson, J. B. (1930). *Behaviorism.* Chicago: University of Chicago Press.

Webster-Stratton, C. (1981; revised 2001). Incredible years parents and children training series. Available from Incredible Years, Seattle, WA: http://www.incredibleyears.com.

Wilson, G. T. (2000). Behavior therapy. In R. J. Corsini & D. Wedding (Eds.), *Current psychotherapies* (6th ed.) (pp. 205-240). Itasca, IL: Fe. E. Peacock.

Wolpe, J. (1958). *Psychotherapy by reciprocal inhibition.* Stanford, CA: Stanford University Press.

3

— ▾▲▾ —

Case Studies of
Behavioral Interventions

In this chapter, case examples illustrate a range of applications of behavioral techniques. Case material brings to light how social workers, rather than directly applying techniques, must often train parents and other professionals who have the environmental control to employ techniques. The examples are interspersed with exercises that reinforce key information to be learned from each case.

EXAMPLE 3-1

Michael, a 23-year-old white male, is a resident of a subacute nursing unit within a long-term care facility because he suffers from muscular dystrophy and respiratory failure. Michael is dependent on a mechanical ventilator to assist with his breathing. He is also extremely obese. Michael's nurse, Alison, reported to the facility's social worker that she was having a difficult time with Michael's care and that he was often noncompliant.

Assessment

When asked about specific problem behaviors, the nurse said Michael frequently refused to get out of bed, shower, or allow staff to provide care (such as cleaning his feeding tube and skin). He also was resistant to efforts to assist in weight loss, which would greatly improve his quality of life. Michael engaged in verbal sparring matches over aspects of his care, and eventually the staff would give up. Other than his mother, who came for weekly visits, the social worker found out that Michael only had contact with the medical staff. The social worker then interviewed Michael about the quality of his care. As an explanation for his refusal to cooperate in his care, he said he "just didn't feel like it" and that "it was too much trouble."

Exercise 3–1

At this point, do you have a hypothesis about how Michael's problem behaviors are being maintained? What intervention strategy might be used based on your hypothesis?

Goal-Setting

In a meeting with the client, Michael, and his nurse, Alison, the social work intern, helped them come to an agreement about handling Michael's care. Together they formulated the following goals:

1. Michael will get out of bed two times per week.
   - He will initiate conversation with staff to discuss when he would like this activity to take place

- When staff requests that Michael move his arm or leg to assist with the process, he will comply within 5 to 7 seconds
- Michael will remain out of the bed and in his wheelchair for a minimum of 3 hours before requesting to get back in bed
2. Michael will take a shower once a week.
3. Michael will allow Alison to clean feeding tube and surrounding area once per week.

Intervention

The social worker explained to Michael that there were to be no more arguments about his care. If he refused medical attention, then staff would accept his wishes and leave the room. However, if he accepted care, then staff would spend time with him. When Michael had reached his three stated goals, he would be allowed to choose a video rental to watch in his room.

The next meeting involved the social worker, Alison, and the two nurse aides who were primarily responsible for Michael. The purpose of the meeting was to train them on behavioral techniques. First, they were taught how to make effective requests in a polite and non-demanding manner, stating the presence of positive behaviors rather than the absence of negatives, and to make such requests as specific as possible. (For example, "Michael, please raise your arm," or "Michael, please lift your head so that I can wash your hair" rather than saying "Stop resisting.") They were then taught praise and ignoring techniques. For the latter, the social worker instructed Alison and the nurse aids to simply leave the room without further comment or acknowledgment of any outburst on Michael's part. Or, if their duties required them to remain in Michael's room to complete a task, they were not to engage him in conversation and were to keep a neutral facial expression.

One of the nurse aides responded that he believed these techniques would simply make Michael mad. His comment gave the social worker the opportunity to share with them the likelihood that initially Michael's noncompliance might increase before it decreased. She explained that this was called an extinction burst, a common occurrence when first attempting to employ extinction, and that they should not give up. She further explained that extinction would not be effective if it was not applied in a consistent manner.

Evaluation

After the first week, Alison reported that Michael had only met one part of his three goals: he had gotten out of bed once and stayed up for 3 hours. Alison reported that she and her staff had been able to praise and ignore, but that it was a struggle at times (see Chapter 8 for further information on this case).

The social worker, having learned of Michael's desire for a haircut, suggested that they add in the possibility of another reward and make a haircut contingent upon Michael's first taking a shower. Michael needed to have his hair washed in order to go to the barber shop for a haircut. The social worker arranged with the facility to cover the cost of the haircut.

Exercise 3-2

What else could have been done with Michael's behavioral plan when he met so few of his goals?

The following week, Alison said that she and her staff had applied the extinction model fairly consistently and employed the use of praise on a regular basis. Michael had met two out of his three goals. The possibility of a haircut had successfully motivated him to take a shower and wash his hair. Alison further reported that Michael was so thrilled with the haircut that he got out of bed the next day so he could "show it off." She also revealed how glad she was to have been warned about Michael's possible reaction to the extinction model.

> *Alison:* It was awful there for awhile. I felt like Michael was refusing treatment just out of spite. It really was difficult to stick with it. In fact, it was just in the last two days that he took a shower and got out of bed! Prior to that he wouldn't do a thing! For awhile I was thinking that I wouldn't have anything good to report this week.
>
> *Social worker:* But you stuck with it, and I'm so proud of you. Remember, this is an ongoing process. Ups and downs will be a normal occurrence in the next several weeks.

Alison was so pleased with the outcome of the haircut that she wanted to use another tangible reward and had already come up with an idea for the following week. The respiratory therapy department was planning a weekend "movie night" (showing a series of videos) for the vent-dependent patients. The purpose of this activity was to increase socialization among patients and to provide an incentive for patients to leave their rooms. Thus, for the next week, Michael would have the opportunity to earn two rewards, the first being movie night, the second being a movie rental of his choice if he met all three goals.

The following week, Alison happily reported that Michael had met all his goals. Over the next several weeks, the social worker gradually phased out her help to Alison as Alison and her staff became more adept at handling Michael's challenging behaviors. In response, Michael became much more compliant with his medical care.

EXAMPLE 3-2

Krista, 6 years old, and Molly, 4, live with their parents, Peter and Cassie Brewster. Krista recently completed kindergarten and Molly attends daycare. Due to the summer break, both girls are currently attending daycare on a full-time basis. Both Krista and Molly have difficulties at daycare. They cry and do not want to participate in activities.

Peter and Cassie reported that when Krista was a toddler and learned to climb out of her crib, she began to come into their room nightly. Within the last 2 years, Molly has begun to do the same. Because of this situation, everyone is tired in the morning, which results in Peter and Cassie running late for work (they are both employed full-time). They believe that if the girls were getting a better night's sleep, then their behavior would improve at daycare and there would ultimately be less stress among family members.

Assessment

The social work student elicited more specific details about the behavioral sequences. Peter and Cassie described an example of a typical night, which includes Krista getting out of bed at around 1:30 a.m., then Peter or Cassie taking her back to her room. Cassie gets into bed with Krista until Krista falls back to sleep. Shortly thereafter, Molly comes into her parents' bedroom, then Peter or Cassie takes her back to her room. This continues several times throughout the night. Peter travels regularly with his job, so Cassie often handles this situation on her own. Cassie admits that sometimes she is just too exhausted and simply allows the girls to sleep in her bed.

When asked what corrective measures they had previously attempted, Peter and Cassie replied that they usually began by making idle threats, such as removing TV privileges, bedtime stories, or trips to McDonald's during the week. When this approach seemed to fail, they resorted to screaming at the girls and at each other ("If you get out of bed one more time, you will not watch TV for a week!"). Both parents realized some of their threats were unrealistic for both them and their children.

Exercise 3-3

What is your hypothesis of how this behavior originated and how it is being maintained?

Goals

The ultimate goal was for Krista and Molly to remain in their beds for the entire night on a consistent basis. Peter and Cassie decided that bedtime should start at 9 p.m., and the girls were not to come out of their rooms until a parent came to get them at 6:30 A.M.

Intervention

As Peter and Cassie seemed to have some understanding of the concept of reinforcement, the social work student explained to them in more detail that when used correctly, it can be an effective means of increasing a desired behavior. The student further explained that when trying to develop or change a behavior, they should begin by reinforcing each occurrence of the desired behavior. After the desired behavior becomes more consistent, reinforcement can then be provided on an intermittent basis to maintain the behavior. He explained that praise is one type of reinforcer, which can be both easily given and used in conjunction with more concrete types of reinforcers.

> *Social work student:* On mornings when one or both girls has gotten out of bed the night before on only two occasions, this seems to be a step toward our goal. What can you do to reinforce their behavior when they get out of bed twice instead of three times?

> *Cassie:* I guess we could tell them how proud we are that they stayed in their beds for as long as they did.
>
> *Social work student:* Very good. I'm glad you remembered what I mentioned earlier about being specific with praise and talking about what you want—staying in bed—rather than what you don't want.
>
> *Peter:* Yes, but I just don't like praising them when they continue to get out of bed.

In answer to Peter's concern, the student said that it would be necessary to include other more concrete types of reinforcement to increase the desired behavior. Peter admitted, "At this point, I'm not sure if anything will work to keep them in bed, but I'm willing to try."

The social work student suggested using stickers, which could be pasted on a chart: one sticker would be provided for getting out of bed two times, two stickers for getting out of bed once, and three stickers for not getting out of bed at all. Further, values could be placed on the stickers to be redeemed for rewards. After discussion of what type of rewards would be motivating for their children, the parents decided that one sticker could be exchanged for a piece of candy, two stickers would allow them 15 more minutes in the pool, and three stickers would be a video rental. They used these rewards because they were things they tended to give the children anyway. Now they would be contingent upon earning stickers.

Exercise 3-4

Do you have any comments or suggestions at this point about the reinforcement system that has been set up?

The student inquired about any potential problems that would prohibit them from carrying out this system. Peter said, "Since I'm not always home, I tend to spoil the girls by bringing them candy and other surprises when I return from a trip. Won't this weaken the value of the rewards?" The student commended him for thinking about this and asked him how he could incorporate the surprises he brought home into the reward system. Peter decided that he would give them to the girls once they earned their three stickers.

Cassie stated that a problem for her was being firm with the girls when sending them back to their rooms. The girls would caress her face and tell her how much they loved her when they came into her bed at night. "Many times, I'm too tired to take them back to their bed, so I just move over and let them sleep with us. I have even tried asking them if they would be more comfortable in their own bed, and of course their reply is always 'no.'"

The social work student thought this was a good time to discuss command giving. He explained that commands in the form of questions are not effective, as children will often say "no" in response. Instead, it was important for Cassie to specifically state what she wanted them to do. He also told the couple about "when/then" commands (e.g., when they stayed in their beds, then they could get stickers in the morning). Likewise, Peter and Cassie could praise the girls for compliance to a command. For example, as the girls are returning to their own bedroom, Peter or Cassie could say, "Molly, you are doing such a good job of going back to your bedroom when I asked you to. Thank you."

At this point, the girls were invited back into the room so that Peter and Cassie could explain the new sticker system. They seemed to understand how they could earn prizes with their stickers and expressed excitement about playing this new "game."

Evaluation

The social work student began the next session by reviewing progress toward the goal. Cassie stated that it had been helpful in the goal-setting process to set a standard bedtime of 9 p.m. She realized they had not previously been clear with the girls—sometimes they were allowed to stay up until midnight; other times they were put to bed at 9:30. Peter stated that "at first, both girls threw a fit about the new bedtime schedule, but then they eventually agreed." When they were asked how they handled this situation, Peter replied that he told the girls, "Remember, girls, this is part of earning your stickers." Since this seemed to work, the student decided that they would not have to revise the system to provide another sticker for going to bed.

Peter and Cassie stated that the first few nights did not seem encouraging for Molly, who continued to get out of bed and come into their room three or four times, whereas Krista immediately began to work toward earning her stickers. Cassie said that "even though Krista still got out of her bed and came into our room, she only did so twice during the night, instead of her usual three times."

As laid out in the plan, Krista earned her sticker for both days and was given a piece of candy.

Cassie reported that Molly became very upset about not getting a piece of candy and began crying. Peter said this was extremely difficult for him to bear, "especially when Molly started saying that she didn't love us anymore because we loved Krista more than her." Peter went on to say that after Molly calmed down, "we explained to her that we will always love both her and Krista equally, no matter what. We then reminded her that the reason Krista got some candy and she didn't was because she had not earned any stickers yet for staying in her bed. When she did, then she could also have candy." The student complimented Peter on being able to remind Molly of the system in a loving manner and for using the words "yet" and "when," which communicated that he was confident Molly would earn stickers, as well.

The student also reminded the couple about their previous threats to remove privileges from the girls without following through. The student explained, "It seemed like Molly was 'testing the waters' because she probably didn't believe you would really make her earn the rewards." Peter and Cassie, smiling, agreed.

Peter and Cassie described that this event seemed to have sparked a bit of competition between the girls. After being reminded of the reinforcement system, Molly said to them, "I'm gonna get more stickers than Krista because I'm gonna stay in my bed all night." On the third night, Molly stayed in her bed the whole time, and Krista got out of bed only once. The fourth and fifth nights also proved to be successful: Molly got out of bed once and Krista remained in her bed on both nights.

In subsequent contacts, Peter and Cassie reported that they had continued to use the sticker charts and reward system, and each night, the girls were getting out of their beds on a less frequent basis. Peter and Cassie admitted that it felt "odd" that the girls were not coming into their room at night. In fact, on one occasion, they quietly got out of bed to check on the girls "just to make sure everything was okay."

The daycare workers commented to Peter that the girls had not been crying as much as they used to and that they also seemed more willing to participate in activities with the other children. Peter and Cassie attributed this to the girls' getting better sleep. Likewise, Peter and Cassie reported getting more sleep and being on time for work, which helped with their stress levels considerably.

Peter's only concern at this point was whether they "would have to keep doing the stickers and rewards forever." The social work student explained that once the girls remained in their beds on a consistent basis, then the reinforcement could be gradually reduced and eventually eliminated. To begin reducing the reinforcement system, he suggested that Peter and Cassie provide stickers for staying in bed all night as opposed to continuing to earn stickers for each effort made. When this was achieved, they could gradually move to removing the daily use of stickers and provide a reward only at the end of the week for remaining in bed every night. Finally, the reward could be phased out.

Peter asked what they should do if the reinforcement system was eliminated, and one or both of the girls came into their bedroom. First, the social work student reminded Peter that they should continue to praise the girls for staying in bed at night and refuse to allow the girls in their bed if they should come into their room, giving them a command to return to their own beds. If these efforts did not work, they could reintroduce the reinforcement system for a short time.

EXAMPLE 3-3

This case involves an intervention in a nursing home initiated by the social work intern and implemented by the nursing staff. Before she entered the nursing home, 80-year-old Mrs. Moran suffered a fall and broke her hip. Since living there, she has a fear of walking to the bathroom by herself because she is afraid she will fall again. This problem has caused Mrs. Moran to request wearing protective undergarments, which in turn leads to arguments with the nursing staff, sometimes lasting up to an hour. They tell her that if she wets herself in the undergarment, it could lead to urinary tract infections and skin breakdown. Plus, she needs to get up to walk for her exercise.

The head nurse calls Mrs. Moran's adult son, who says he doesn't know what he can do about it, since he's not there. He agrees to speak with his mother, saying, "Now, Mom, you know it's not good for you to go in the diapers. You need to go down the hall to the bathroom." However, his talking to Mrs. Moran does not impact her behavior in the least.

The head nurse believes that Mrs. Moran carries out this behavior for attention: "She is a very sweet lady. She loves to have you talk to her. It's just that we're so busy, it's impossible for us to spend one-on-one time with all of the residents twenty-four hours a day. She sees that some of the residents are a lot worse off than she is, like Mrs. Atkins across the hall who needs total care from us. I think Mrs. Moran wants to be helpless so she can have that extra attention."

Exercise 3-5

What is your assessment of the situation in terms of behavioral principles?

Exercise 3-6

What is your plan for intervention?

The social work intern explained in a meeting with Mrs. Moran, her son, the head nurse, and the nurse aides that from then on, the nursing staff would agree to Mrs. Moran's request for protective undergarments. They would no longer argue with her about it; they would help her on with the diapers in a matter-of-fact way, doing so as quickly as possible without chit-chat. If Mrs. Moran instead requested help to go down the hall to the bathroom, two aides would assist her and would spend time talking with her, as long as this did not go over 15 minutes.

As a result of this plan, Mrs. Moran became fully compliant with getting up to go to the bathroom. Her cooperative behavior was reinforced with attention and time with the staff. Her insistence on wearing adult diapers was extinguished because staff no longer engaged in discussions about the topic.

EXAMPLE 3-4

The social work student, who was placed in a preschool intervention program, worked with a 4-year-old African American girl on her frequent use of swear words in class. The preschool teacher, Ms. Bickham, talked to Malika about her language, but it didn't change Malika's behavior. The social work intern assisted Ms. Bickham in addressing the problem using positive reinforcement.

Assessment

The intern first tried to get an understanding of how frequently the behavior already occurred, a baseline of the behavior. Ms. Bickham responded that Malika typically swore about six times a week, or an average of about once per day.

Goal-Setting

The social work student decided that the goal for Malika should be no swear words at all for the week.

Intervention

She talked to Ms. Bickham about setting up the reinforcement system. This involved praising Malika for listening to directions, lying quietly during naptime, staying in her seat during classroom instruction, and remaining in one area during playtime. She then instructed Ms. Bickham to give Malika one sticker at the end of each day that she didn't swear and three stickers if she followed instructions by herself without getting warnings for the entire day. The student intern thought that this system would be particularly effective because Ms. Bickham did not give out stickers in her class. The intern then designed a chart for the teacher to mark Malika's progress from week to week. The intern decided that if Malika were to receive three or more stickers by the end of the week, she would receive a "good behavior" certificate.

Ms. Bickham's current punishment for student infractions was to use time-out in the corner of the room. However, children in time-out could hear the teacher reading stories or doing other types of activities with the other children. The social work intern thought that time-outs might be more effective if they were held in her office, since there was no reinforcement in the office. The intern also thought that the time-out for Malika should be increased 5 minutes for each time that she got in trouble a day.

The next part of the intervention was to explain to Malika what was expected of her and the consequences that would follow. Malika said she didn't want to get in trouble anymore for cursing, and the intern told her that she and her teacher would help Malika with that. When Malika was told about receiving stickers, she said she preferred candy. The social work intern relented and said that Malika could get candy only a few times, and after that, she would be allowed to choose a sticker. Malika was also told about the new system for time-out.

Exercise 3-7

Address some of the problems with the behavioral management plan outlined in Example 3–4, identifying them and then offering solutions.

Summary

In this chapter, examples were taken from school settings, an agency serving the homeless, and medical and nursing care facilities. They provide a sense of the range of settings and problems to which behavioral interventions can be applied. The goal of this chapter was to give you more facility in applying behavioral interventions; appropriately used, they can be very helpful for improving client functioning.

4

— ▼▲▼ —

Cognitive Restructuring

Behavioral theory is focused on *overt* behaviors that can be observed and measured. By the early 1960s, however, the importance of a person's *covert* operations, or cognition, was identified as significant to clinical intervention and added to the theory. This broader focus became known as cognitive-behavioral theory. From the perspective of cognitive theory, conscious thoughts are the primary determinants of feelings and behavior (Beck, 1995). Thoughts are referred to by many names: cognitions, self-statements, beliefs, attitudes, appraisals, assumptions, attributions, attitudes, perceptions, expectations, schemata, and scripts (Azar, Barnes, & Twentyman, 1988; Dobson & Dozois, 2001).

Many mental, emotional, and behavioral problems are the result of cognitive misperceptions—conclusions that are based too much on habits of thought rather than on external evidence—that people have about themselves, other people, and their life situations.

These misconceptions may develop for a couple of reasons. The first is the simplest: the person has not acquired the information necessary to manage a novel situation. This is often evident in the lives of children and adolescents. They face many situations at school, at play, and with their families that they have not experienced before, and they are understandably not sure how to respond.

The other source of misperception is rooted in personal *schemas*, or systematic patterns of thinking, acting, and solving problems, that are too rigid to manage new situations. Because of their tendency to develop thinking habits, people often interpret new situations in biased ways. These patterns are generally functional—all people utilize cognitive distortions at times—and they only create difficulty when they become too rigid to allow for the input of new information. Table 4–1 includes some widely held cognitive distortions, also known as irrational beliefs, as identified by Beck (1976). Conversely, "rational" thinking can be understood as thinking that is based on external evidence, is life preserving, keeps one directed toward personal goals, and decreases internal conflicts.

TABLE 4–1 Common Irrational Beliefs

Irrational Beliefs	Examples
Absolute thinking: viewing events in all or nothing way	"Since I know I can't win if I play tennis with my friend, I might as well not play at all."
Catastrophizing: seeing minor situations as disastrous	A date doesn't call back: "I'm never going to get married."
Low frustration tolerance: inability to put up with minor inconveniences or uncomfortable feelings	Waiting for a stoplight: "This is driving me crazy. I'm never going to get to where I'm going."
Overgeneralization: drawing the conclusion that all instances of some kind of situation or event will turn out a particular way because one or two did	"I went to that one support group in L.A. when I lived there and that group didn't help. Therefore, I won't go to any other groups because they won't help either."
Personal worthlessness: a specific form of overgeneralization associated with failure	An individual is worthless if the house isn't spotless.

Source: A. T. Beck, *Cognitive Therapy and the Emotional Disorders*. New York: Guilford, 1976.

The nature of change in cognitive-behavioral theory is apparent in its hyphenated term. That is, clients can be helped to change in three ways (Young, Weinberger, & Beck, 2001):

- Cognitively, by teaching them how to identify and change distorted thinking.
- Behaviorally, by offering skills training to improve coping capability.
- Experientially, by helping clients set up natural experiments so they can test the extent to which their beliefs about an event are rational.

In the latter two ways, new skills and experience lend themselves to more adaptive thinking.

Cognitive interventions focus on present rather than past behavior (Leahy, 1996). The past is important for discovering the origins of a client's thinking patterns, but it is present thinking that motivates behavior. The nature of the social worker–client relationship is important because it must catalyze the client's difficult process of questioning basic assumptions and considering alternatives (Mattaini, 1997). The social worker must demonstrate positive regard for the client while alternately functioning as a model, coach, collaborator, and trusted representative of objective thinking. The social worker is active, participating in discussions and in the mutual development of change strategies.

In clinical assessment, the social worker assesses the client's schema, identifies faulty thinking patterns or cognitive deficits, and considers the evidence supporting the client's conclusions about his or her life situations. When those conclusions seem valid, the social worker initiates a process of problem solving or teaches coping skills (see chapters 6 and 7). When the conclusions are distorted, the social worker utilizes techniques to help clients adjust their cognitive processes in ways that will better facilitate goal attainment. The social worker guides the client through the process, but the client is responsible for implementing these strategies. As thinking changes, so do emotions and behaviors.

Cognitive Restructuring

Cognitive restructuring was formulated from two different schools of cognitive therapy: rational-emotive therapy (Ellis & McLaren, 1998) and cognitive therapy (Beck, 1976; Beck & Freeman, 1990). Both schools share the assumption

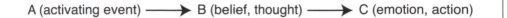

A (activating event) ⟶ B (belief, thought) ⟶ C (emotion, action)

Figure 4–1 ABC model of cognitive restructuring.

that problematic reactions result from interpretations of situations that are often negative or illogical (as described in Table 4–1).

In *cognitive restructuring*, the social worker assesses the client's patterns of thinking, determines with the client that some of them are not effective for managing important life challenges, and through a series of discussions and exercises, helps the client to experiment with alternative ways of approaching challenges that will promote goal attainment (Emery, 1985).

In rational-emotive therapy, the ABC model of cognitive restructuring is used (see Figure 4–1). ABC represents cognitive processing in which A is an activating effect, B is a person's belief about the event, and C is the consequence of A and B for the person (emotion and then actions).

People often assume that A directly causes C, but closer examination shows that a cognitive event, B, intervenes between the two. For instance, if A is an event that occurs (a teen asks her mother at the last minute if she can go to the mall, and mom says no), and C, the consequence, is the teenager's sulking, then B (belief) might be, "My mother never lets me do what I want." If the same activating event (parent refusal) occurs, and the resultant emotion (consequences, or C) is understanding, the belief might be, "I shouldn't have waited until the last minute. Next time if I really want to go, I'll make sure to ask in time."

Exercise 4-1

The following practice examples involve situations with teenagers. To help you become more adept at identifying intervening beliefs and formulating alternative beliefs, please give some possibilities in the space provided for each example. Obviously, at times, you will have to make some assumptions about each case in order to come up with a response.

1.

    Event: Jeans are a little tight.
Thoughts: I'm fat and disgusting. If only I were thinner, I'd be happier.
Feelings: Worthlessness, self-disgust.

2.

    Event: Teen looks through fashion magazine and sees pictures of slim models.
Thoughts: If only I were thin like these women, then I'd be happier.
Feelings: Depression.

3.

    Event: A day when a few things went wrong.
Thoughts: This day was so bad, I'm just going to get drunk and forget about it all.
Behavior: Get drunk.

4.

    Event: A party.
    Negative thought: "I need drugs or alcohol to feel better."
    Behavior: Use drugs or alcohol.

5.

    Event: A party.
    Negative thought: "Everyone uses marijuana. It can't be that bad."
    Behavior: Use marijuana

6.

    Event: Something doesn't turn out the way a teen wants.
    Negative thought: "I wish I was never born."
    Consequence: Depression.

7.

Event: A boy the teen likes doesn't show any interest.
Negative thought: "I'm too much of a loser for him to like me."
Consequence: Depression.

8.

Event: A guy the teen likes is pressuring her for sex.
Negative thoughts: "I really like him. If I don't do this, I'll lose him, and he'll find someone who will have sex with him."
Behavior: Gives in, loses self-respect.

Exercise 4-2

Consider your own recent experience. Construct an ABC sequence for a negative response or feeling you have had. Substitute a more appropriate belief into the sequence. How did that change your response?

Steps of Cognitive Restructuring

In order to change a client's belief systems, four steps are necessary. These include working on the following with the client:

- Providing information on the connection between thoughts and feelings.
- Identifying the thoughts.
- Examining the validity of the beliefs.
- Replacing the irrational or problematic thoughts with more functional thoughts.

Connection Between Thoughts and Feelings

The first step in cognitive restructuring is to educate the client on the connection between thoughts and feelings with statements such as, "Let's take a look at what you've been saying to yourself. Are you aware that your mind is constantly generating messages? There's a constant running commentary in the background of our minds. These thoughts we're having influence how we feel and act, even though we might not be very aware of them at first. But we actually have more control over these than you might think, and it is one way that we can directly influence the way we feel and act."

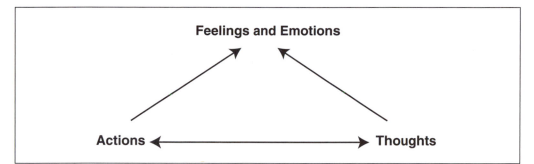

Figure 4–2 Visual diagram showing the connections between feelings, thoughts, and actions.

Visual diagrams on the connections between feelings, thoughts, and actions may also be useful; see Figure 4–2. For example, if a person feels depressed, she may not feel like getting out of bed. Staying in bed (the behavior) may then cause her to feel even worse (she is not getting done what she needs to). Thoughts and actions are also interrelated in the same way. For example, if the same person thinks, "I don't feel like getting up, but staying in bed is just going to make me feel worse. I'm going to get up and get stuff done. That will probably help" those thoughts might result in her getting out of bed and accomplishing tasks. Her productivity may, in turn, influence the thoughts she's having (e.g., "Now that I'm up, it doesn't seem so bad. At least I'm getting stuff done"). A sense of accomplishment and more positive thoughts may lead her to experience a boost in mood.

Clients are educated that cognitive-behavioral therapy works on each of these domains. *Actions* are changed by building skills in the areas of social skills, problem solving, communication, assertiveness, and so on. They work on changing *thoughts* by stopping irrational thoughts and increasing positive thoughts. They work on changing *feelings* by changing their thoughts, changing their actions, and learning relaxation skills. Cognitive restructuring specifically focuses on working to change thoughts so that they are more positive and realistic.

Exercise 4-3

Considering a recent example from your life, describe the interconnection between feelings, thoughts, and behaviors.

EXAMPLE 4-1

Monisha Jackson was a single mother of two girls with sickle cell anemia. The social work intern introduced the idea of cognitive restructuring to Ms. Jackson as a technique to help her manage anxiety about dealing with her daughters' disease.

> *Social work intern:* This process starts by your becoming aware of your thoughts right before and when you are anxious.
> *Ms. Jackson:* I told you, I just feel real anxious, that's all.
> *Social work intern:* Yes, you have said that you feel real anxious. What I'm talking about now, however, is the things that you *say* to yourself. You probably say them to yourself almost automatically, so you sometimes don't even realize you're thinking or saying these things.
> *Ms. Jackson (tentatively):* Okay, if you say so.
> *Social work intern:* These thoughts, or things you say to yourself, affect what you feel and what you do. So, if

you can discover the things that you say to yourself
that keep you feeling anxious, you might be able to
keep from feeling anxious by changing those thoughts.

Ms. Jackson: Anything that works. I'll try anything. You help
me figure out my thoughts *(chuckles)*, then I'll try to
change them to feel better. You just have to help me
along because I'm a bit confused.

Social work intern: Okay, I'm glad you're willing to do this.
I think it might help.

Identifying the Thoughts

After educating the client, the second step involves helping the person identify
the thoughts preceding and accompanying the distressing emotions and non-
productive action ("What was going through your mind . . . ?"). Some clients
may require more tangible ways to grasp their thinking patterns (Cournoyer,
2000). They may be asked to engage in imagery work ("Close your eyes, take a
deep breath, and see yourself in that situation. What are you doing? What are
you feeling? What are you thinking?"). The social worker may invite other
clients to participate in a role play. By re-enacting a problematic situation, some
clients can more easily retrieve the thought patterns maintaining the problem.
Clients often confuse thoughts and feelings, and indeed, in speech, people often
use the terms interchangeably. However, cognitive restructuring requires one to
differentiate between the two. A couple of examples follow on helping clients
elicit their cognitions. The first shows how the social work intern helps Ms. Jackson, from Example 4–1, recognize the thoughts that trigger her feelings.

EXAMPLE 4-2

Social work intern: Now I want you to close your eyes.
(Pause.) Picture yourself in your kitchen, where your
calendar is. You look up and see that a week has gone
by since Toya [youngest daughter] has been in the
hospital. Now tell me everything that you're thinking.

> *Ms. Jackson:* I'm getting tight just thinking about it. (*Puts her hand on her chest.*) I guess I'm thinking, "Here we go again. They're going to get sick again, and I'm not going be able to handle it. They're going to go to the hospital and never come home. (*Speech quickens.*) I'm thinking that I should be sick instead of them. They're going to get sick and know that their momma did this to them, that their momma made them feel this pain, and hate me because of it."

In the next example, a social work student helps a client identify a distorted belief that lies behind his tendency to be financially victimized by others.

EXAMPLE 4-3

Malcolm is a 36-year-old African American man diagnosed with paranoid schizophrenia. Malcolm is easily taken advantage of by others. The student asked him to recall a specific incident that resulted in Malcolm sending the telephone company a check for $300.

> *Social work student:* What were you thinking when you said yes to the salesperson's request for the money?
>
> *Malcolm:* I knew I didn't understand the plan she was talking about. But I didn't want to ask. I didn't think she would tell me the truth anyway.
>
> *Social work student:* What were you thinking would happen if you did ask her?
>
> *Malcolm:* She would probably think I was stupid.
>
> *Social work student:* So, you're on the phone with her and you say yes to her request because you're afraid to ask what she's talking about?
>
> *Malcolm:* Yeah.
>
> *Social work student:* And you're afraid to ask because she might think you are stupid?

Examining the Validity of the Beliefs

After the beliefs have been identified, they are examined for their validity. The different ways of establishing whether or not a belief is valid include

- examining the evidence
- considering an alternative perspective
- looking at the worst-case scenario
- point-counterpoint
- scaling interventions
- didactic teaching
- experientially, by helping clients set up natural experiments so they can test the extent to which their beliefs about an event are rational.

These methods are detailed in the following text. Worksheets accompany the various methods for your use with clients.

EXAMINING THE EVIDENCE

Examining the evidence involves asking the client to provide evidence for and against the distorted belief and is the most common way of uncovering the validity of thoughts (McKay, Davis, & Fanning, 1997). The social worker may pose a series of questions for the client to consider:

- When did the feared outcome not happen in the past? What was different about those times? What was the client thinking and doing differently?
- What are the odds of the feared outcome occurring?
- How many times in the past has the catastrophe actually happened?

Because it is the most common way of examining the evidence, several examples are provided in this section.

EXAMPLE 4–4

Maya is a 42-year-old Russian woman currently living in northern Virginia. Maya moved from Yugoslavia to the United States approximately 10 years ago with her husband and son. Maya now has two children, is college-educated, and is employed full time at a small professional company. Maya and her family recently became involved with child protective services after her husband was criminally charged with sexually abusing their 5-year-old daughter. Maya has been supportive of her daughter and expresses anger toward her husband; she is against future reunification. During this caseworker's client contacts, Maya presents as extremely anxious and lacking confidence in her ability to cope with the current crisis as well as with daily stressors.

The child protective services caseworker inquires about the probable odds of an event happening that the client is worried about.

> *Caseworker:* You've mentioned that you frequently worry about losing your job, right?
>
> *Maya:* Yes. I mean, things are fine now with money and everything, but I don't know what will happen if I lose my job. I can't imagine what I would do.
>
> *Caseworker:* What do you think the chances are, out of 100 percent, that you'll lose your job?
>
> *Maya:* I don't know, maybe 40 percent.
>
> *Caseworker:* Is there a reason that you might be fired or laid off?
>
> *Maya:* No, but I have been missing work lately.
>
> *Caseworker:* I can imagine that it must be scary to suddenly be the only breadwinner for your family. Is your supervisor aware of the recent situation with your family?
>
> *Maya:* Yes, they know. They've been very supportive.
>
> *Caseworker:* Okay, has your supervisor mentioned to you that he's concerned about the work you've missed?

Maya: No, I have sick days to use.

Caseworker: Has your performance at work deteriorated in any way recently that would cause your job to be on the line?

Maya: Not really. I know I probably don't deserve to lose my job, but you just never know.

Caseworker: Well, how many people do you know who have lost a job for no apparent reason?

Maya: None, I guess.

Caseworker: So what do you think the chances are of your losing your job for any reason within the next year?

Maya: Probably close to zero. (*Breathes.*) I guess that's probably not going to happen.

Through a series of deductive questions, the caseworker was able to help the client see that her thoughts were unrealistic, and the client seemed to experience a decrease in anxiety as a result.

In examining the evidence, a social worker may also gather evidence with the client about instances of behavior that negate the client's belief, as in the next example.

EXAMPLE 4-5

A social work intern worked with a mother, Viola, who was HIV-positive and had recently lost custody of her 15-year-old son to the child protective services system. Viola had not been able to follow through with making the call to the substance abuse treatment center that she had been court-mandated to attend, and she had not rescheduled an appointment she had missed at a job training center. Viola said, "What's the use of doing any of these things? I'm a failure. Especially as a mother."

Social work intern: What makes you think that?

Viola: Because I screw everything up.

Social work intern: You don't think you can do anything right as a parent.

> *Viola:* Well, no, I do some things right.
> *Social work intern:* Like what?
> *Viola:* Um . . . (long pause) like getting John to the dentist last
> week.

The social work intern and Viola then compiled a long list of good
things Viola had done as a parent within the past month or so.

This exercise is akin to the solution-focused approach of focusing on
exceptions to the problem, times when the problem either is not present or
when it is reduced in frequency or intensity (O'Hanlon & Weiner-Davis, 1989).
Focusing on when the problem is not a problem often reduces the dichotomous
thinking that sometimes afflicts people when they are embroiled in problems.

As a result of her conversation with the social work intern, Viola felt
much more empowered and resolved to make the necessary calls. She also recognized that her thoughts of failure were keeping her stuck (e.g., "If I'm a failure, what's the point in doing anything to improve my situation? I'll mess that
up, too").

Recall again the example of Ms. Jackson, the mother of the two children
with sickle cell anemia.

EXAMPLE 4–6

> *Social work intern:* Let's start with the first statement. You
> said that your daughters are going to get sick again,
> and you won't be able to handle it.

Exercise 4-4

How would you go about helping Ms. Jackson refute the belief that she won't be able to handle it if her daughters get sick again? Write your responses here and then read on to see how this intern handled the refutation process.

Social work intern: As you have noted, your daughters get sick a lot, and as you know, sickle cell is a chronic disease, so, yes, they might get sick again. [Here the social work intern acknowledges the reality of the illness and the girls' condition.]

Social work intern: Who takes care of the girls when they get sick?

Ms. Jackson: I do.

Social work intern: Always?

Ms. Jackson: Yes, from the time they were itty-bitty things, I always have been the one to take care of them. I give them their medicines. I take them to the hospital. I stay there with them. I hold them when they feel pain. No one else is going to do it.

Social work intern: So have you ever "not been able to handle it" when they were sick?

Ms. Jackson: No, I guess I've been able to handle it okay.

Social work intern: Just okay? Do you think someone else could work with your daughters in a better way than you do when they get sick?

Ms. Jackson: No, I know them, and I know just what they need and how to do it. I know that spot on Toya's back that I can massage and make her feel better. I know that my other daughter likes warm milk when she's in pain. A mother knows these things. *(Smiles.)* I know these things.

Social work intern: Excellent. You have now proven that what you said before, "They're going to get sick again and I'm not going to be able to handle it," is not totally true. Yes, they might get sick again, but you have told me that, indeed, you can handle it.

Ms. Jackson: Yeah, I guess so. *(Smiles.)*

Exercise 4-5

What statements might you make at this point and what questions might you ask to help Ms. Jackson refute the belief that her daughters are going to get sick and "know that their momma did this to them, that their momma made them feel this pain, and hate me because of it"?

ALTERNATIVE INTERPRETATIONS OF THE SITUATION

Another way to challenge distorted thinking is to get clients to view the problem from another perspective (McKay, Davis, & Janning, 1997): "What's another way of seeing this?"

EXAMPLE 4-7

Carla is a single mother who is raising two boys, both of whom have been diagnosed with ADHD. She works full time as a secretary and struggles with finding appropriate after-school arrangements for her children. When she talked with the school social work intern, she mentioned feeling like a "bad mother" because her boys were getting poor reports from school due to their conduct and grades. The social work intern asked her about an alternative view, and this mother was able to say, "Actually, all I do is for my kids. I work so I can give them a decent life, and so they can see someone working for a living rather than going on welfare. I help them with their homework in the evening even though I'm tired. I try to teach them right from wrong." She concluded that perhaps she wasn't a bad mother after all.

The social worker may also offer a *reframe* in order to help a client get an alternative perspective. Reframing is one technique by which the practitioner introduces people to a new way of viewing the problem (Bertolino & O'Hanlon, 2002). Through reframing, individuals are introduced to a novel way of viewing some aspect of themselves, others, and their problem or situation.

Clients who suffer from cognitive distortions often view themselves differently from how others experience them. Asking relationship questions to get clients to perceive themselves from someone else's perspective may help them see themselves more realistically (de Jong & Berg, 2001): "How would your mother say you have been doing since you returned home?" "What would your girlfriend say about your drinking now?" With such questions, clients are challenged to appraise themselves more appropriately through the viewpoints of other people (de Jong & Berg, 2001).

WORST-CASE SCENARIO

This type of questioning confronts the cognitive distortion of catastrophizing. One purpose in asking about worst-case scenarios is that it gets the client to realize that the feared negative consequences about a situation are often not as dire as the client assumes (McKay, Davis, & Janning, 1997). Recall Example 4–3 regarding Malcolm, the man with schizophrenia, who struggled with resisting pressure from salespeople. The social work student asked him, "Let's say the woman on the phone does think you're stupid if you don't go along with her. Does it matter?" Malcolm thought for awhile and said, "I guess it wouldn't matter. Why do I care if she thinks I'm dumb?"

Asking about the worst-case scenario also helps the client to cope if the worst fear comes true. The social worker can ask such questions as, "Realistically, how long is the experience likely to last? How can you manage during that time?" The social worker might then train the client on coping skills or developing another plan. For example, a social work student worked with a mother who was afraid to tell her daughter about her HIV status. To the question, "What's the worst that can happen?" the mother replied that her daughter might tell her friends at school and they might start teasing her daughter. Since this was certainly a possibility, plans were discussed for how her daughter could keep this information private from her friends.

Another way the worst-case scenario can be used is to take it even further to exaggerate the situation to the point of absurdity. ("So there you are, having fainted away in front of everyone from anxiety, then what happens?") Humor is often the response to such absurdity, which acts to diffuse some of the intensity of the thoughts.

POINT-COUNTERPOINT

An additional way to work with client distortions involves using point-counterpoint. In this technique, the costs and benefits to the client for maintaining certain attitudes are covered (Young, 1990). By partaking in this exercise, clients begin to get a sense that beliefs and cognitions are not as fixed as they once thought, and the very process of exploring beliefs allows their thinking to become more flexible.

EXAMPLE 4-8

This example involves Kate, a 24-year-old Caucasian female, who had been admitted to the hospital. Kate was 26 weeks pregnant and had been binging and purging throughout her pregnancy. As a result, she had not put on the necessary weight she needed for her baby's growth. In the hospital, she was put on a feeding tube so that her own and her baby's nutritional needs were met. When she met with the social work intern, they talked about Kate's binging and purging and the beliefs underlying this behavior. One of Kate's beliefs was: "If I gain weight, then I'm a disgusting slob." They went through the advantages and the disadvantages of the belief.

Advantages of having belief

I maintain a low weight.
I feel better about myself.
I won't lose control and become fat.
Other people won't think I'm huge.

Disadvantages of having belief

My baby doesn't grow properly and might be born deformed or
    harmed in some way.
I have to be hospitalized even though I have no money or insurance
    to pay for it.
I feel guilt for what I might be doing to this child.
If I gain weight now, I can lose it after the pregnancy, but if my child
    is born with a problem, both of us might have to live with it for
    the rest of our lives.
When I binge and purge, I do lose control.
I have to be on a feeding tube because I haven't gained enough
    weight for the pregnancy.

On balance, Kate said that she realized that, for the sake of her child, she has to gain weight during the pregnancy. Obviously, given the seriousness of the problem, many other interventions must be called into play, and Kate will need to be closely monitored for at least the duration of her pregnancy in order to ensure the safety of her child.

SCALING INTERVENTIONS

Another way to work with negative belief systems is through the use of scaling interventions. The negative belief is anchored at 1, and the opposite, more functional belief at 10. This alternative belief system is made concrete by asking the client to name the actions and thoughts that accompany such a belief. The gradations of the scale and the concrete rendition of a continuum help people loosen their hold on the dichotomized thinking that underlies cognitive distortions and leads to problem behaviors. The steps for using the scale are the same as those outlined in Chapter 1.

- Construct a scale of the belief phrased as a positive statement.
- Identify behavioral anchors at 10.
- Have client rate self in relation to the scale.
- Ask client relationship questions.
- Set tasks involving moving up the scale in 10 percent increments.
- Monitor the client's progress on the scale.

EXAMPLE 4-9

A victim services social worker received a referral from a police officer who had worked the scene of a domestic dispute involving a single mother, Vera, a 35-year-old Caucasian, and her 16-year-old daughter. The officer reported the mother as distraught to the point of being suicidal. By the time the social worker arrived to assist, the daughter had agreed to stay at a friend's house for the night so that mother and daughter could "cool off."

Vera kept crying and saying that "life isn't worth living." Although she said she felt like dying because of the pain, she was not going to kill herself and didn't have a plan. Vera had four children and was raising them alone with only government benefits to support them. The social worker first helped Vera construct the belief in terms of a positive statement. The social worker drew a scale from 1 to 10 and asked, "What is the opposite of the belief you now have that life isn't worth living?" With additional questions and prompting, Vera eventually came up with "Life is worth living."

In the next step, the social worker probed for behavioral anchors at 10, asking Vera, "What will you be doing when you have the belief that life is worth living?" It took some time for Vera to grasp the questioning, in part because it implies that the positive belief is indeed a possibility through concrete action. Vera responded that 10 means "I will be attending college, my children will be listening to me, and I will have a boyfriend." Often, clients select anchors that are removed from their own actions. For example, "I will have a boyfriend" is to some extent outside of the client's control because it is dependent on the actions of others. Therefore, the social worker explored this further, asking Vera, "What types of things will you be doing when you have a boyfriend?" She said, "I will be going out dancing and having fun and have someone to spend time with in the evenings and on weekends." The social worker then used *those* activities as behavioral anchors for 10 instead of "having a boyfriend."

Vera rated herself a 3 on the continuum of having this belief. The social worker, reacting with amazement, asked Vera what she had done to get herself to that point. "Well, sometimes my kids listen to me, at least the younger ones do," Vera explained. "And just having my kids—well, I can't kill myself because of them."

In the next step, the social worker asked Vera relationship questions. She knew from their previous conversation that Vera was close to an aunt who lived nearby, so she asked Vera, "Where would your aunt rate you on this scale that life is worth living?"

"Oh, she would say a 10. She says I have my health, and I have these healthy children, and that's what really counts. And she says that she cares about me and would be devastated if I wasn't around, so that would mean my life must be worth living."

Finally, the social worker asked how Vera could make a 10 percent change (one movement on the scale) between now and the next time they had contact. Vera decided that getting her two teens to listen to her more would help her feel a lot better and that life was worth living. At this point in the contact, the social worker and Vera discussed some behavioral management strategies (see Chapter 2).

At the next contact, the social worker asked Vera where she was on the "life is worth living" scale. She reported that she was at a 4. She'd been able to get her teens to do some chores around the house, and the place was looking better, which helped her mood. During the contact, they talked about how Vera could socialize more—inviting a friend to go dancing, for instance, or going out to the park on the weekends so she could meet some other parents with children. They also talked about a step Vera could take toward her goal of attending college, which was to call the local community college and ask for an informational packet. The work continued in this vein, and Vera eventually moved to an 8 on the "life is worth living" scale before she decided that she felt better enough that she didn't have to have further contact with the social worker. (See Figure 4-3.)

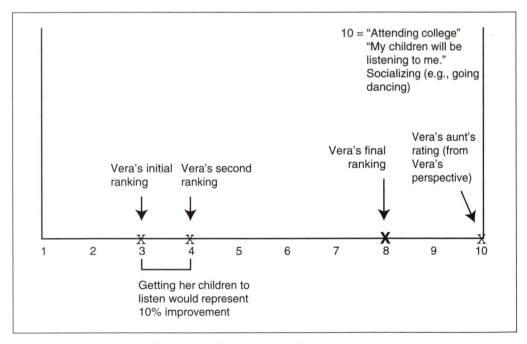

Figure 4–3 Vera's "Life is worth living" scale.

DIDACTIC TEACHING

Didactic teaching means filling in information gaps for clients (Bandura, 1977). The assumption is that cognitions (information) affect the way people feel and behave. For instance, many mothers, when faced with the sexual abuse of their children, are frustrated with them for not telling sooner about the abuse. This frustration sometimes compromises the support that is so necessary for a child's recovery from sexual abuse. Social workers who work with such cases provide parents with information on this dynamic, offering some of the possible reasons children do not tell: the perpetrator threatens the child; the child does not want to get the offender in trouble; the child fears being blamed or punished if the abuse is discovered; the child is loyal to the perpetrator; the child fears the effect on the family; the child feels shame, embarrassment, confusion, and helplessness (Deblinger & Heflin, 1996). After hearing about this information, many parents begin to feel less frustrated with their children. This example demonstrates that cognitive understanding can mediate people's feelings in a positive way.

EMPIRICAL INVESTIGATIONS

After using some of the methods already described, another way to refute beliefs is to set up experiments to test the irrational beliefs. For instance, a person who believes that if she goes on a job interview, she will be laughed at, is encouraged to go on a job interview to test this belief. By not having the feared outcome occur, the person begins to chip away at that belief.

Exercise 4-6

Select a belief that creates trouble for you in terms of your feelings or behavior. Choose one of the methods of counteracting negative beliefs and work through the process yourself in one of the worksheets. (Examining the evidence, finding an alternative perspective, and worst-case scenario are detailed in Worksheet 4–1. Worksheet 4–2 involves point-counterpoint, and a blank scale is provided in Worksheet 4–3 for your use in scaling interventions.) What made you choose one method over another? What did you learn about doing this technique with clients? Are there any steps that are unclear to you?

WORKSHEET 4–1   **Methods to Counteract Negative Beliefs**

What is the evidence?

What are alternative ways of looking at this?

What's the worst-case scenario?

WORKSHEET 4–2 **Point–Counterpoint**

Advantages of having this belief	Disadvantages of having this belief
Come up with an alternative belief that serves you better.	

WORKSHEET 4–3 **Scaling Interventions**

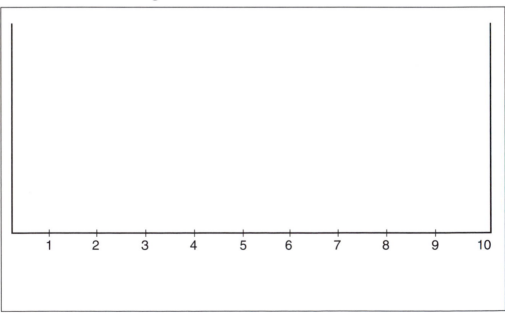

Exercise 4-7

Select one of the ways that you can counteract negative beliefs and work through the process in one of the worksheets either with a client or with another student role playing a client.

Substituting the Thoughts

The final step in cognitive restructuring is to substitute the distorted beliefs with thinking that is more functional. Recall again the example of Ms. Jackson, whose two daughters have sickle cell anemia, and Ms. Jackson's distorted belief, "They're going to get sick again, and I'm not going be able to handle it." After they worked on examining the validity of the belief, the social work intern continued the process of cognitive restructuring by assisting Ms. Jackson in substituting functional self-statements for her self-defeating cognitions. Ms. Jackson decided on the statement, "I've dealt with their illness before, and I can deal with it again. I can do this. I am the best person at taking care of my daughters when they are sick. But right now, they are feeling okay, and so am I." She wrote the statement down, and the social work intern again instructed her to imagine that she was looking at the calendar a week after her daughters were discharged from the hospital. As Ms. Jackson again became anxious, the social work intern instructed her to read her self-statement to herself. Ms. Jackson seemed to relax a bit and smiled in spite of herself.

Exercise 4-8

You have already examined the validity of a distorted belief you hold. Now substitute that distorted belief with a more functional thinking pattern.

Exercise 4-9

Take the statement you worked with in Example 4–2 in which Ms. Jackson says, "They're going to get sick and know that their momma did this to them, that their momma made them feel this pain, and hate me because of it." You already spent some time rebutting this belief. What possible thoughts could act as a replacement for this statement?

Summary

This chapter introduced cognitive interventions that focus on the role of people's beliefs and thoughts and how they can be changed in order to lessen distress and problems in functioning. The process of cognitive restructuring was emphasized, and the steps (educating the client on the connection between thoughts and feelings, eliciting the thoughts, examining the evidence for the belief, and substituting more realistic appraisals) were detailed extensively. Chapter 5 explores the types of problems and populations for which cognitive restructuring is appropriate.

References

Azar, S. T., Barnes, K. T., & Twentyman, C. T. (1988). Developmental outcomes in physically abused children: Consequences of parental abuse or the effects of a more general breakdown in caregiving behaviors? *The Behavior Social Worker, 11*, 27–32.

Bandura, A. (1977). *Social learning theory*. Englewood Cliffs, NJ: Prentice-Hall.

Beck, J. S. (1995). *Cognitive therapy: Basics and beyond*. New York: Guilford.

Beck, A. T. (1976). *Cognitive therapy and the emotional disorders*. New York: International Universities Press.

Beck, A. T., & Freeman, A. (1990). *Cognitive therapy and depression*. New York: Guilford.

Bertolino, B., & O'Hanlon, B. (2002). *Collaborative, competency-based counseling and therapy*. Boston: Allyn & Bacon.

Cournoyer, B. (2000). *The social work skills workbook*. Pacific Grove, CA: Brooks/Cole.

Deblinger, E., & Heflin, A. H. (1996). *Treating sexually abused children and their nonoffending parents: A cognitive-behavioral approach*. Thousand Oaks, CA: Sage.

De Jong, P., & Berg, I. K. (2001). *Interviewing for solutions*, 2nd ed. Pacific Grove, CA: Brooks/Cole.

Dobson, K., & Dozois, D. (2001). Historical and philosophical bases of the cognitive-behavioral therapies. In K. Dobson (Ed.), *Handbook of cognitive-behavioral therapies*, 2nd ed. (pp. 3–39). New York: Guilford.

Ellis, A., & McLaren, C. (1998). *Rational emotive behavior therapy: A social worker's guide*, vol. 2. Atascadero, CA: Impact Publishers.

Emery, G. (1985). Cognitive therapy: Techniques and applications. In A. T. Beck & G. Emery (Eds.), *Anxiety disorders and phobias: A cognitive perspective* (pp. 167–313). New York: Basic Books.

Leahy, R. L. (1996). *Cognitive therapy: Basic principles and applications*. Northvale, NJ: Aronson.

Mattaini, M. A. (1997). *Clinical practice with individuals*. Washington, DC: NASW Press.

McKay, M., Davis, M., & Fanning, P. (1997). *Thoughts and feelings: Taking control of your moods and your life*. Oakland, CA: New Harbinger Publications.

O'Hanlon, W. H., & Weiner-Davis, M. (1989). *In search of solutions: A new direction in psychotherapy*. New York: W.W. Norton & Company, Inc.

Young, J. E. (1990). *Cognitive therapy for personality disorders: A schema-focused approach*. Sarasota, FL: Professional Resource Exchange.

Young, J., Weinberger, A., & Beck, A. (2001). Depression. In D. Barlow (Ed.), *Clinical handbook of psychological disorders: A step-by-step treatment manual* (2nd ed.). New York: Guilford.

5

— ▼▲▼ —

Use of Cognitive Restructuring with Special Populations and Problems

Cognitive restructuring, as we reviewed extensively in Chapter 4, is a major technique in cognitive-behavioral intervention. It can be very effective when applied appropriately, but sometimes students and beginning clinicians have difficulty knowing when to use it. The following guidelines are helpful for determining when cognitive restructuring may be the technique of choice and assessing whether certain populations of clients are appropriate candidates.

You may consider the use of cognitive restructuring when:

- People are distressed by painful emotions or commit behaviors that are detrimental to themselves or to others. When people talk about distressing feelings or problematic behaviors, asking them about the thoughts they were having during these times might uncover some distortions in beliefs. For instance, a woman described that after breaking up with an abusive boyfriend, her stomach became upset, she started shaking, and she felt compelled to call him back. When asked, "What was going through your mind?" the client reported that she was thinking, "What am I going to do? I'm never going to be able to make it without him. I can't do it. Without him, I have nothing." These thoughts were appropriate to target for restructuring because they were preventing her from making a clean break with her boyfriend.

- A client uses "absolutist" language: "never," "always," and "have to." These words signal that possible erroneous beliefs may be operating. In the previous example, the woman said, "I'm never going to be able to make it without him," a clue that a distorted belief was operating its influence.

- A belief system seems to pose a substantial barrier to a client's progress. Recall from Chapter 4, Example 4–3, Malcolm, the young man who was diagnosed with paranoid schizophrenia. The social work intern was working with him on assertiveness, but he seemed to be having difficulty with some of the skills. As a result, the student decided to explore his thoughts during a recent incident in which he had been financially victimized. Only after Malcolm had been through the process of cognitive restructuring was he able to return more successfully to the assertiveness skills training.

- Cognitive restructuring addresses a priority problem for the client.
  In using cognitive-behavioral interventions, the social worker wants to ensure that he or she is using the technique that most appropriately addresses the client's priorities and that targets as many different problems as possible.

We start with a scenario in which you are asked to reflect on this client's circumstances and how best to serve her needs.

EXAMPLE 5-1

Rowena Calvert, a 34-year-old African American mother of three children, lived in a run-down, two-bedroom apartment. Her rent exceeded her ability to pay. Numerous repairs were needed in the apartment, which was part of a Section 8 housing development, but the landlord would not attend to them. To manage her living expenses, Rowena had taken in two boarders.

Rowena had argued with her boarders one night because they took some food that belonged to her. The student involved in the case decided to use cognitive restructuring because of the anger Rowena experienced in this situation and her subsequent "lashing out."

Exercise 5-1

How would you address the client's problems using cognitive-behavioral techniques? Would you use cognitive restructuring? Why or why not?

Exercise 5–2

Consider the guidelines on when to use cognitive restructuring and think about your current or past caseload. Give an example of a case in which it might have been helpful to use cognitive restructuring and explain your rationale.

Box 5–1 Modifications of Cognitive Restructuring for People with Limited Cognitive Functioning

- Present new information slowly and in different ways (say it, show it, do it), and use frequent repetitions.
- Offer shorter, more frequent sessions.
- Ask the client to summarize material more often.
- Use concrete mnemonic devices, such as caricature drawings or other specific visual (e.g., notes written on an index card) and auditory aids (e.g., audiotapes). Tape sessions and encourage people to review them for homework.
- Provide people with folders or notebooks for storing home practice and in-session materials.

Source: K. Laidlaw, L. Thompson, D. Gallagher-Thompson, & L. Dick-Siskin, *Cognitive Behaviour Therapy With Older People*. W. Sussex, UK: John Wiley, 2003.

Special Populations

Are clients who have mental illness or mental retardation appropriate candidates for cognitive restructuring? What about children or the elderly? What about clients who have harmed other people? This section considers each of these special populations and some of the assessments and possible adaptations that the social worker must make to determine the appropriateness of cognitive restructuring. Box 5–1 also covers some modifications to cognitive-behavioral work that can be done when working with people who are limited by their cognitive levels.

Severe Mental Illness

Cognitive-behavioral interventions are often used with people diagnosed with schizophrenia. It is a here-and-now approach, well suited to helping people learn the skills to advance their daily functioning. Several meta-analyses have been conducted on cognitive-behavioral interventions with this population. Pilling et al. (2002) colleagues conducted a meta-analysis of all randomized clinical studies done on cognitive-behavioral interventions for schizophrenia. The researchers concluded that cognitive-behavioral interventions improved clients' mental status and decreased rates of treatment dropout, and that their positive effects persisted through the follow-up period.

The technique of cognitive restructuring requires a client to think in abstract and logical ways. When individuals are actively psychotic, they often cannot distance themselves from their symptoms and are unable to consider other ways of thinking. Therefore, cognitive restructuring can be used with psychotic clients only in areas where their thinking is relatively stable and the client is ambivalent enough to consider other explanations. Better cognitive-behavioral techniques might involve training a client who is susceptible to hallucinations and delusions in thought-stopping and coping self-statements ("I'm okay," "I'm safe"). These are detailed further in Chapter 6. Cognitive restructuring may be appropriate when the client has stabilized. For instance, as demonstrated previously, cognitive restructuring was successfully used with Malcolm. The social work intern was also able to teach Malcolm and other clients diagnosed with schizophrenia to recognize different cognitive errors and to apply them to their own experience outside of any hallucinations or delusions they had.

Mental Retardation

For clients diagnosed with mental retardation, behavioral therapy tradition-ally has been the main approach, but as the wide range of abilities, functioning levels, and individualized responsiveness to specific techniques has become recognized, a variety of treatment approaches have been successfully used, including cognitive-behavioral therapy.

Because mental retardation is not a finite illness with a specific set of symptoms universal to everyone with the diagnosis, it becomes difficult to universalize the treatment approach. Each person should therefore be individ-ually assessed for his or her ability to respond to cognitive-behavioral tech-niques. In general, these techniques are best suited for those with the cognitive abilities to process and understand the approach. For those with mild mental retardation in particular, cognitive-behavioral therapy is recommended as a first-line treatment for some co-occurring mental disorders, including major depressive disorder, posttraumatic stress disorder, and obsessive-compulsive disorder (Rush & Frances, 2000).

EXAMPLE 5-2

Steve, a middle-aged white male, is diagnosed as having mild mental retardation. Steve lives at a residential program and is employed outside the agency for five days a week. Steve recently suffered a spinal cord injury, which forced him to depend on a wheelchair for mobility. Prior to his injury, Steve was physically active, taking many walks around the agency's grounds and play-ing basketball in the gym. He also enjoyed spending time with the other residents and liked going to movies, unit parties, and other activities. However, since the injury, Steve has withdrawn from nearly all social contact and spends most of his day sleeping.

The social work intern spoke with Steve about his reactions, asking him several questions to ascertain the reasons behind his lack of participation. Steve said he was too much of a bother for staff because he was the only one in a wheelchair and required more attention than the others, who could walk around by themselves. The intern asked him how he knew this. After thinking for a moment, he said, "I don't know. No one ever said anything, but it takes them a lot of work to get me in and out of this thing"— indicating the wheelchair—"and someone has to be with me the whole time so they can push me around."

After more questioning, Steve admitted that staff must not be thinking he was so much of a bother because they regularly asked him if he wanted to join in on activities. He agreed to test his belief and participate in one outing before the next time he saw the social work intern. He was then to share his thoughts and reactions with her.

When he met with the social worker, he agreed that going out with the others had helped him feel better. He reported that the staff did not indicate he "was a bother," and seemed happy that he was joining them.

Children

Cognitive-behavioral techniques are routinely used with children, but as you know by now, cognitive-behavioral therapy comprises a potentially wide range of techniques to employ, including problem-solving, self-instruction, self-talk, and social skills, among others (see chapters 6 and 7), rather than just cognitive restructuring. For cognitive restructuring specifically, cognitive abilities should be sufficiently developed to enable shifts in thinking about the past and the future, to follow logic, and to grasp abstractions.

In Durlak, Fuhrman, and Lampman's (1991) meta-analysis on the use of cognitive-behavioral therapy with youth, level of cognitive development was a central factor in the results. The effect of intervention for children ages 11 to 13, who are presumably functioning at the formal operations stage, was about twice that of children ages 5 to 11. However, young children are often participants in cognitive-behavioral interventions, and indeed, cognitive-behavioral therapies are supported by the research literature with effectiveness indicated for a number of different problems and disorders (McCellan & Werry, 2003). Methods may have to be adapted through artwork, analogies, and puppets (e.g., Webster-Stratton & Hammond, 1997). Many resources for cognitive-behavioral work with children are listed in the appendix.

The Elderly

Cognitive-behavioral interventions have been most often used with elderly clients for the treatment of depression, but also of anxiety (Laidlaw et al., 2003). A review of studies on therapy for depression in the elderly showed that cognitive-behavioral therapy was consistently more effective than usual-care or wait-list control groups, and that treatment gains persisted over time (Arean & Cook, 2002).

The social worker should be aware of several phenomena when working with the elderly as described by Laidlaw and colleagues (2003). The first is the common belief among the elderly (and the general population) that depression is a normal part of the aging process rather than a disruption in functioning. Elderly clients often make comments about being old as if it is synonymous with depression and being decrepit and incompetent " . . . rather than an indication that they hold ageist beliefs and have set up an expectancy bias for themselves where they expect to be unhappy because of their age." These beliefs therefore are appropriate targets for cognitive restructuring. The elderly may also have to be educated about the potential capacities that people with old age possess. Laidlaw et al. (2003) recommend *Successful Aging* (Rowe & Kahn, 1999) and the informational brochure *Ageing: Exploding the Myths* (WHO, 1999).[1]

With the elderly, it is also often necessary to address some cohort belief systems about accepting help. These beliefs have to do with discussing problems outside the family and the presumed "failure" or "weakness of character" associated with being unable to handle problems on one's own. If the elderly person does not verbalize these concerns, the social worker may need to bring them up for discussion; otherwise, they might act as a barrier to the older adult's getting help.

---

[1] World Health Organization (1999) Ageing: Exploding the Myths, accessed at HTTP://www. who.int/hpr/ageing/publications

The older person is typically used to being a patient in the medical model; therefore, the social worker must help the client understand the collaborative nature of cognitive-behavioral interventions and must encourage feedback. Likewise, the social worker will have to explain the necessity of homework, which may be either a foreign or antiquated notion for an elderly client.

The social worker should further be aware that extensive storytelling about the past is common among elderly clients; indeed, older adults often expect that they should provide this level of detail to a person offering assistance. To address this phenomenon, the social worker should describe cognitive-behavioral therapy as a structured and time-limited approach. To keep to time limits, a "ground rule" may need to be set up so that the social worker is allowed to interrupt a prolonged bout of sharing and redirect the client to the topic at hand.

Finally, in working with elderly clients, the social worker should be sensitive to possible sensory and cognitive limitations. Written information provided must be in a font large enough for the person to read. If writing is painful because of arthritis or other conditions, an alternative means of doing homework may be necessary, such as tape recording. If the client has memory problems, the social worker can record salient points of the session, provide handouts, and jot down homework assignments for the older adult to refer to later. Laidlaw and colleagues (2003) further emphasize that cognitive-behavioral treatment can be used with the cognitively impaired elderly person, although goals need to be modest in nature, steps should be simplified, and contacts kept short.

The following example of cognitive-restructuring with an elderly person takes place as part of a social work intern's hospital placement.

EXAMPLE 5-3

Velma Barnes, an 82-year-old Caucasion female, is on the orthopedic floor of a city hospital. She broke her leg earlier in the week and is awaiting surgery to reset the bones. Because she is on a blood thinner, she has to wait 48 to 72 hours from her last dose before she is ready for surgery. During this timeframe, Mrs. Barnes became increasingly worried about her future. A referral was placed to the social work student to assist Mrs. Barnes with her discharge planning.

When the social work student met with her, Mrs. Barnes was teary and soft-spoken. She expressed concern for her future because she will be unable to live independently and has no one to take care of her upon her discharge from the hospital. She also talked about her sadness and stress over her son being a widower and raising his daughter alone. Until now, she had been a support resource for him, helping him take care of his daughter. She now perceives her situation as being burdensome to her son, not only leaving her unable to assist him but requiring him to help her instead.

While listening to Mrs. Barnes express her desolation, the social work student empathetically reflected her feelings of concern and sadness. When Mrs. Barnes seemed to have calmed somewhat, the social work student asked her if they could talk about her plans for discharge. Mrs. Barnes agreed and quickly shared her worst fear—that she will have nowhere to go.

In order to help the client gain a realistic appraisal of the situation, the social work student asked Mrs. Barnes if she thought that having nowhere to go was a likely outcome. Mrs. Barnes had to agree that it was not. Mrs. Barnes then returned to the topic of feeling like a burden to her son. The social work student asked how her son was reacting to her upcoming discharge. Mrs. Barnes said he was in the process of preparing his house for her to come live with him. However, it would still take some time for the house to be ready to accommodate her physical needs.

Given the cognitive-behavioral assumption that information delivered cognitively will help with people's distress, the social work student informed Mrs. Barnes of some other options in the meantime, involving short-term community placements (nursing homes). Mrs. Barnes's mood seemed to lighten once she learned that there were some places she could go. But she started crying again, saying she was still concerned about being a burden to her son.

The social work student then turned to deductive questions to ask Mrs. Barnes what she had done to help her son since his wife's death several years prior. Mrs. Barnes spoke at length about how she helped him raise his daughter and cooked and cleaned for them. When she finished outlining her various supportive activities over the years, the social work student asked if she thought it possible that her son was looking forward to being able to help her in return for the support she provided him. Mrs. Barnes agreed it was possible, saying that they had become very close since his wife's death.

The social work student then inquired about the evidence that Mrs. Barnes's son was feeling burdened by having her move in. Mrs. Barnes had to admit that he had been nothing but helpful and supportive. The meeting concluded with a discussion of how Mrs. Barnes could focus on accepting his help rather than being consumed with worry that he felt burdened by her. Mrs. Barnes's mood improved considerably, and she expressed relief about having met with the social work student to help sort out her concerns.

People Who Harm Others

When clients' actions have been harmful to others, the social worker must be careful not to use cognitive restructuring so that it rationalizes what the client has done. However, cognitive restructuring may be helpful when the client has taken responsibility for his or her behavior and desires change. At this point, cognitive restructuring may be very effective for assisting the client to see the thoughts and rationalizations that are fueling inappropriate behaviors. For example, a person who has been violent with others might have irrational thoughts such as, "I have to hurt people who disrespect me." A client who has been sexually abusive of children might have thoughts such as, "It's not really harmful what I'm doing. I'm just being a friend to this child." These types of thoughts are suitable targets for cognitive restructuring.

EXAMPLE 5-4

An example involves Mikhail, a Russian immigrant to this country, who was admitted to a psychiatric hospital when he tried to commit suicide. He'd divorced his wife 3 years before after a 17-year marriage. The loss of this relationship, among other factors (he'd lost his job because of his depressive symptoms), was playing into his depression. In the hospital, he reported to the social worker that he kept thinking, "It's all my fault, it's all my fault." When she asked him what this meant specifically, he said, "I wasn't very good at talking out problems, particularly about the children. My wife thought I was too authoritarian." Further conversation revealed that he had struck his wife while they were married, and she'd had a protective order issued against him.

Exercise 5-3

How would you address the client's problems using cognitive-behavioral techniques? Would you use cognitive restructuring? Why or why not?

Crisis Intervention, Grief and Loss, and Trauma

Social workers often see clients as they experience a loss (e.g., death, romantic break-up, physical injury), stress (e.g., isolation, illness, eviction), or trauma (e.g., crime, sexual assault, child abuse, violence). In such situations, the social worker listens to the client's account of what has happened in an empathic way that conveys validation and support. Listening empathetically often represents the bulk of the social worker's response. Cognitive restructuring may not be necessary; it is certainly not used to rationalize clients out of feelings that are natural to have in the circumstances. Indeed, cognitive restructuring should not be used until the client has been validated for his or her experience and feelings related to the situation *and* a distorted belief has presented itself. A way to differentiate between normal stress, loss, or trauma reactions and faulty beliefs may include a statement to the client such as the following: "Your sadness is perfectly natural given what has happened, and the tears are a normal part of the grief process. I wonder, though, when you are saying, 'I know now that no one will love me again.' Can we look at that a little closer?"

One way of combating dysfunctional beliefs that may inhibit a person's recovery is providing direct reassurance or information that counteracts the negative belief. An example follows from a victim services setting:

EXAMPLE 5-5

A social worker employed in a police department was talking with two victims who had been in a convenience store robbery a couple of hours before. The clerk (a woman) and the customer (a man) were watching the surveillance tape to see if they could add to the description of the perpetrator. After viewing it, the man turned to the social worker and said sheepishly, "I look like a chicken." (He had hit the floor when the robber brandished a gun and said, "Everybody down.") The social worker quickly noted that an erroneous belief was operating and provided immediate reassurance, stating that the customer might have been killed if he hadn't followed the robber's directive, and she might not be talking to him now! The important thing was that he was alive, and there was nothing much he could have done against a gun. He nodded and relaxed, seemingly reassured by her statements. Before he left the police station that night, she checked in with him again about what he was thinking, and he said, "It's like you said. I don't know what I could have done. And I'm alive—that's the main thing."

Because the area of crisis intervention, grief and loss, and trauma is so large, we continue with some longer case examples that you can read and reflect upon, either by yourself or as part of class discussion. The following two examples are drawn from hospital social work in which people have to cope with serious illness (first case) and injury (second case). Passages of dialogue are included so that you can better understand how the practitioners in these examples used deductive questioning to help examine the validity of the client's beliefs.

EXAMPLE 5-6

Paula, a 35-year-old white female, was diagnosed with amytropic lateral sclerosis (ALS), also known as Lou Gehrig disease, approximately 5 months ago. Paula depends on a ventilator for her breathing. Because she no longer has control over her body functions or the use of her arms and legs, she relies on others for all her self-care needs.

She and her husband have two children, ages 9 and 11, who live at home with their father. Not surprisingly, Paula reports difficulty coping with the progression of her disease and frequently cries during visits with the hospital social worker, who provides empathy and validation of her experience. Lately, Paula has mentioned that she feels like "a failure as a mother."

The dialogue between the social worker and Paula centers on eliciting the cognitive messages underlying Paula's feelings:

Social worker: You say you feel like a failure as a mother. What's going through your mind when you say that?
Paula: Things like, "I'm not with them often enough, and how can I be a good mother when I'm lying here in this bed and can't even get up?" I just feel so helpless. I'm failing them as a mother. I'm not there when they go

off to school in the morning. I'm not there when they come home.

Social worker: So what I hear you saying is that because you're not physically there with your children at home every day, you're a failure as a mother?

Paula: Yes, that's right.

Social worker: Do you really believe that?

Paula: Yes, sometimes.

Social worker: But not all the time?

Paula: No, because I can't help it that I'm like this. I would be at home if I could be.

Social worker: How would you describe a "good" mother?

Paula (smiles): Someone who loves their children and would do anything for them. Someone who's always there for them. And if they're hurt or sad, someone they can talk to. A child always needs to know they can come to their mother with anything. I think that's important. It's also important that someone teaches them right from wrong.

Social worker: Which of those things do you do for your children?

Paula: I try to squeeze in as much as I possibly can. My husband brings them by most days. On the days he can't bring them here, we talk on the phone.

Social worker: So you do see your children fairly regularly? You talk to them, spend time with them when they're here?

Paula: Of course.

Social worker: And have your children ever indicated to you that they think you're not there for them or that you're a bad mom?

Paula (smiles): No, but I know this is hard for them.

Social worker: I know how difficult this is for all of you.
    (*Allows for silence while Paula cries. After a few moments, Paula continues.*)

Paula: But we're all doing the best we can, given the circumstances.

Social worker: What does your husband have to say about all of this? Does he think you're a failure as a mother?

Paula: No, he says I'm doing a good job.

Social worker: Well, let's look back at your original thought, "I'm a failure as a mother." Given the questions I've asked and your responses, what evidence do you really have that you're a failure as a mother?

Paula: None, I guess. It's just the way I feel sometimes.

Social worker: Do you feel that way right now?

Paula: Well, no, not really.

Exercise 5-4

In the conversation between Paula and the social worker, what steps did the social worker take to work with Paula's belief that she was a failure as a mother?

Exercise 5-5

What is the line between validation of Paula's loss of physical capacities and using cognitive restructuring? (This may be a good topic for class discussion.)

EXAMPLE 5-7

The intern in this example was placed in a hospital setting for her field placement. He was asked to talk with a 26-year-old woman, Emma, whose hand had been so badly injured in a traffic accident that it had to be amputated. Her ribs had also been broken.

Before her accident, Emma had led an active life, working as a researcher for an employees' rights organization and living with her friends in a rented apartment in the downtown area. A volunteer for many nonprofit organizations and an active vegan, Emma frequently was involved in protests for social justice issues.

In the hospital, the nurse at morning rounds said that Emma was crying constantly. A psychiatrist had evaluated her and had recommended an antidepressant. Emma adamantly refused this recommendation, stating that she did not want to "feel like a zombie" as a result of the medication.

The student was primarily involved with discharge planning at the hospital and had a heavy caseload. Therefore, he had only about 30 minutes to spend with this client during the first contact.

Emma: (Starts crying after the intern introduces himself.) Well, I'm sure you know what's happened to me. Did the nurse tell you how they sent a psychiatrist in because I couldn't stop crying? He didn't even ask me why I was crying. I think he thought it was because I was in so much pain. Well, it wasn't. I feel utterly worthless now. It's funny how things happen—one minute you're driving to work, next thing you know, you're in the hospital and missing your hand. Everything has changed, and I just cannot deal with it.

Social work intern: It's natural that you are sad. You've gone through a tremendous loss. A lot of what you're feeling is grief for what you've lost.

Allowing some time for Emma to express her feelings, the social work intern provided some information about the grief process: that Emma would continue to feel sadness, and perhaps other emotions, such as anger that she had to go through this and at the person who caused the accident, or fear as she remembered what it was like to be in the accident and how she was going to live her life now. The emotions, although difficult, were part of the natural process of grief.

Emma nodded her understanding and then went on:

Emma: It's not the physical pain that's getting to me. I've gotten used to it. I just feel absolutely useless.

Social work intern: Tell me what you mean by that.

Emma: Well, my friends and I signed up for a bicycle charity ride. This cause is very important to me, and I really wanted to take part in this race. Now I can't do it. I used to volunteer at the free clinic too, and I can't do that now either.

Social work intern: So you're saying that you feel useless because you can't do your part to help out?

Emma: Yes, I mean I know these people from the clinic. I want to help.

Social work intern: You think you're letting people down?

Emma: That, and other things. I can't go with friends to the peace rallies either. I feel strongly about these issues and can't do anything about it.

Social work intern: So you think that because you cannot physically participate in the ride or these demonstrations, you have let people down and are not doing your share. And if you can't do all that, what use do you have?

Emma: Exactly.

At this point, the intern discussed the role of thoughts and emotions, saying that Emma had more control over her thoughts than over her feelings. When Emma was thinking that she was useless and had no right to accept help, those beliefs were hurting rather than helping her, and she could replace those thoughts with some that were more reasonable. The intern gained Emma's permission to examine more closely her belief that she was useless if she didn't participate in social justice activities and in helping people.

Social work intern: What evidence do you have for this?

Emma: Well, nothing specifically. Come to think of it, my friends are the ones coming to see me now instead of the other way around. They are the ones asking me if I need anything. I'm not used to that. I'm always the one helping others, not vice versa. *(Starts crying again.)* I've never had to ask for help before. I'm pretty self-reliant.

Social work intern: Can you think of reasons your friends would want to help you?

Emma: Well, I'm a good friend, and I have always stood by my friends and helped them out. One of them got arrested at a protest last year, and I bailed him out of jail.

Social work intern: You *are* a good friend! Can you think of other reasons that your friends and family would want to help you?

Emma: They feel sorry for me.

Social work intern: What's another way to see this?

Emma: I don't know. That's the way I see it.

Social work intern: I wonder if the offers to help are not meant to make you feel useless, but rather a way of people saying thank you for the help you have given them in the past.

Emma: I never really thought of it that way, but yes, maybe.

Social work intern: So what can you say to yourself instead?

Emma: I've helped out other people. I guess now it's my turn to need help. It won't always be this way.

Social work intern: Very good!

Before the session ended, the social worker assigned Emma some homework. Learning that Emma's family had brought her a tape recorder, the social work intern suggested that anytime Emma caught herself having distorted beliefs, she should record herself and then state an alternative thought. Emma grasped the idea quickly.

The social work intern also wanted to evaluate their work. He posed a 1-to-10 scale, "with 1 meaning you were feeling utterly awful, and 10 meaning you are feeling fine. Then he asked, "Where were you on the scale when we started talking today?" Emma responded, "Definitely a one!" When the intern asked about where Emma would place herself at the end of their time together, she said she was at a 3. "This has put things in a better perspective."

Exercise 5-6

What is your opinion of how this student handled the client's feelings and the crisis she is experiencing? This question is posed as a topic of discussion rather than as a problem with only one right answer.

Exercise 5-7

What irrational or negative beliefs did Emma present in her conversation with the social work intern?

Exercise 5-8

Which beliefs did the intern target for intervention in this example?

Exercise 5-9

What methods did the intern use to help Emma refute her beliefs?

Exercise 5-10

What is your opinion about the way the social work student carried out his evaluation of his work with Emma? Note that this exercise may be appropriate for a class discussion on this issue.

The next day, when the social work intern stopped by, Emma said that she had done her homework and that she was now at a 4 on the scale.

> *Emma:* But I still have these lingering feelings of being useless. My parents brought me up to be pretty self-reliant and to set challenges for myself. Last year, I hiked the Appalachian Trail; now I can't even go to the bathroom by myself.
>
> *Social work intern:* You're saying that your parents instilled in you the value of being independent. That's fine, but you seem to be saying that you should be fully independent now, and since you're not, you should feel bad about yourself.
>
> *Emma:* Although it sounds silly put like that, I have been feeling that way.
>
> *Social work intern:* What would your parents expect of you in this situation?
>
> *Emma:* What do you mean?

Social work intern: Do you think they would expect you to do everything that you used to do for yourself?

Emma (laughs): Of course not.

Social work intern: And yet, this is the biggest challenge you've faced. Certainly bigger than the Appalachian Trail.

Emma: That's true.

Social work intern: Do you think they want to help you face this challenge, with the things that you can't do for yourself yet?

Emma: Yes, if I asked.

Social work intern: Okay, then I've got another assignment for you. While your parents are here, ask for help on three different occasions. Something like, "Mom, could you help me up to go to the bathroom?" "Dad, can you take me down to the sunroom and sit with me for awhile?" The reason I am asking you to do this is not to make you utterly dependent on your parents, but to challenge your belief that you have to be independent and self-reliant all the time.

The social work intern ended the contact by asking Emma to rate herself once more on the 10-point scale. At this point, Emma reported that she was a 5.

Exercise 5-11

What process did the intern use to help Emma refute her negative belief in this conversation?

In their third and last session before Emma was to be discharged, the social work intern again began by asking about the assignment. Emma responded that she had found the home-work hard but that she had done it. She asked her father to help her brush her teeth and her sister to take her to the bathroom. She rated herself a 6 on the scale.

> *Social work intern:* A six. I am impressed. Since you will be transferred to the rehab hospital tomorrow, this will be our last session. You'll be doing a lot of work there and will really be challenged, and you'll have ample opportunity to ask for help.
>
> *Emma:* Yes, it should get easier for me, but with all the bad things that have happened, I'm really afraid I'll start getting depressed again.

In response, the intern encouraged Emma to keep tape recording her negative thoughts and countering them with more realistic statements. He also suggested that Emma continue asking for help at least three times a day. Finally, the intern talked with Emma about working with a therapist on a regular basis if these tools were not enough to help her manage. Emma said that it was good to know further help was available if she should need it.

Summary

The final section of this chapter focused on the topic of grief, loss, and trauma and how cognitive restructuring can play a role in that work. The case illustrations demonstrated the need for careful assessment by the social worker to determine the normal reactions a person would have to a particular crisis, stressor, or trauma and when dysfunctional beliefs might be inhibiting the process of recovery. Properly applied, cognitive restructuring can be very helpful for people coping with these types of difficult situations.

The overall purpose of this chapter was to provide some guidelines for the social worker on when to appropriately use cognitive restructuring. Various types of populations and problem areas that the social worker may encounter were highlighted, and information was provided on how to assess whether a particular problem may lend itself to the technique of cognitive restructuring.

References

Arean, P., & Cook, B. (2002). Psychotherapy and combined psychotherapy/pharmaco-therapy for late life depression. *Biological Psychiatry, 52*, 293–303.

Durlak, J., Fuhrman, T., & Lampman, C. (1991). Effectiveness of cognitive-behavior therapy for maladapting children: A meta-analysis. *Psychological Bulletin, 110*, 204–214.

Laidlaw, K., Thompson, L., Gallagher-Thompson, D., & Dick-Siskin, L. (2003). *Cognitive behaviour therapy with older people.* W. Sussex, UK: John Wiley.

McClellan, J., & Werry, J. (2003). Evidence-based treatments in child and adolescent psychiatry: An inventory. *Journal of the American Academy of Child and Adolescent Psychiatry, 42*, 1388–1400.

Pilling, S., Bebbington, P., Kuipers, E., Garety, P., Geddes, J., Orbach G., & Morgan, C. (2002). Psychological treatments in schizophrenia: I. Meta-analysis of family intervention and cognitive behavior therapy. *Psychological Medicine, 32*(5), 763–782.

Rowe, J., & Kahn, R. (1999). Successful Aging. NY: Dell.

Rush, A. J., & Frances, A. (Eds.). (2000). Expert consensus guideline series: Treatment of psychiatric and behavioral problems in mental retardation. *American Journal on Mental Retardation, 105*, 159–228.

Webster-Stratton, C., & Hammond, M. (1997). Treating children with early-onset conduct problems: A comparison of child and parent training interventions. *Journal of Consulting and Clinical Psychology, 65*, 93–109.

6

— ▼▲▼ —

Cognitive Coping Skills

Coping skills, broadly defined, are tools that help individuals manage and negotiate stressful events. The emphasis is on the client learning new behaviors; skills are learned, just as problem behaviors were learned. We divide coping skills into those that are cognitive in nature and those that are based in behavior, and we devote one chapter to each. Included in this chapter are the techniques of self-talk, self-instruction training, thought-stopping, and coping with craving.

Self-Talk

Self-talk is a process by which people can build an internal cognitive framework for instructing themselves in how to cope effectively with problem situations (Meichenbaum & Deffenbacher, 1988). It is based in part on the premise that many people naturally engage in internal speech, giving themselves "pep talks" to prepare for certain challenges. Further, when people find themselves in difficult situations, those that evoke tension or other negative emotions, their thinking may become confused, and their ability to cope diminishes.

Clients instead are trained in self-talk skills so that they can:

- arm themselves to approach stressful situations: "I'll be okay—this is just a problem to be solved," "It's okay to feel nervous, but I can deal with this."

- manage the event as they are experiencing it through coping statements: "I'm doing just fine," "I'm nervous, but I'm getting through it," "It'll be over soon."
- give themselves reinforcement afterward: "I did a good job," "That was tough, but I stuck to it," "Next time it'll be even easier." (Meichenbaum & Deffenbacher, 1988; Spiegler, 1993)

EXAMPLE 6-1

Paula, the patient with Lou Gehrig disease (see Example 5-6), said that she sometimes has difficulty breathing and grows panicky while waiting for the respiratory therapist to assist her. When the social worker asked her what thoughts ran through her mind, Paula described statements such as "They're never going to get here," and "I can't breathe, I can't breathe." The social worker then modeled some alternative self-coping statements that Paula could use instead: "I know the therapist is on his way; he always comes," and "I can breathe, I am breathing now, and I will continue to breathe." Next the social worker had Paula repeat the coping statements. The social worker also modeled self-reinforcement statements for Paula: "I am coping with this situation," "I am doing a good job," "I am getting better at this," and "That wasn't so bad." Each time, Paula repeated the statements after the social worker.

The social worker then asked Paula to talk about another event that caused her anxiety. She responded that she often felt anxious while she was waiting for the nurse to come and clean her after a bowel movement. The loss of control of body functions was especially difficult for Paula. She tended to blame herself while she waited, saying things like, "If I had called for a bedpan in time, this wouldn't have happened. I should have known this was coming." These types of statements only increased her distress.

The social worker modeled coping statements and asked Paula to repeat them aloud: "I know that this is going to happen sometimes; the nurse will be here just as soon as she can," "It can't be helped—I am going to cope with this situation," "Stay calm for just a little longer. I can do this," and to reinforce herself afterward, "That wasn't so bad. I'll do even better next time."

Exercise 6-1

Consider an upcoming stressful event (say, a test or a presentation in one of your classes or a contact with a challenging client) and develop a plan for self-talk coping that takes into account how you will approach the event, how you will cope during the event, and how you will reinforce yourself afterward.

Exercise 6-2

Consider a client you are seeing and a stressful event he or she faces on a regular basis (parenting, job interviews, etc.). Hypothetically, create a self-talk coping plan that takes into account how the client will cope and reinforce himself or herself before, during, and after the event.

Self-Instruction Training

Self-instruction training is a technique in which the client and practitioner develop a step-by-step self-instruction script following their completion of a plan for confronting a problem. Preparing an internal or written script for stressful situations can help a client recall and systematically implement the coping strategy previously selected. Self-instruction training has been studied mainly in relation to children and school task completion, but it can also be taught to adults (Spence, 1994).

Such a script may be written down or memorized by the client. The social worker and client visualize and walk through the problem situation together so the client can rehearse its implementation. The client then uses the script in his or her natural environment either before or during an assigned task.

EXAMPLE 6-2

Rowena (whom we met in Example 5-1) had difficulty talking to her landlord about making repairs on her apartment, so the social work student helped her develop a self-instruction script as follows:

"I'm not putting it off any more. I have a right to ask for these repairs. I'm walking across the courtyard, feeling confident that I can do this. When he looks at me and says, "What do you want?" I say, "I need to talk to you about some repairs." I am very calm, knowing I have a perfect right to do this, and I need to do this so my children and I can live better. When he says, "Can you come back later?" I take a deep breath and say, "No, I need to talk to you about it now. I've already put these requests in before, and there hasn't been any response." I don't have to raise my voice, but I'm very firm and confident.

I then tell him the list of repairs that need to be made: I need the toilet to flush right, the back door deadbolt replaced because it fell off, the heat vent fixed, and the outlet in the kitchen to be fixed, since right now we have exposed wiring coming out, which is a danger to the children.

When he says he'll get to it, I ask him when will that be. I am still very calm and firm, because I know I have recourse if he ignores me again. I thank him for his time and start walking back, proud of myself for going down there and doing what I need to do."

As the social work student wrote down the steps, they discussed the challenges that might come up, such as the landlord acting rudely and discouraging Rowena from making requests. The social work student, in the script, kept the focus on Rowena and her responses rather than on what the landlord might do. After the script was completed, Rowena read it through. A few times her breathing become short due to anxiety. The student had her breathe calmly for a few moments and then resume. Rowena read it through a few times until she no longer felt anxiety doing so. After several practice runs through the script, she said she felt prepared to talk to the landlord and made a commitment to do it the next day.

Exercise 6-3

Consider a task that is onerous or difficult for you (for example, starting a paper for school). Create a self-instruction script that takes into account the individual steps of the tasks and includes the coping statements that can be inserted along the way.

Exercise 6-4

With a fellow classmate, role play a client–social worker situation and have the "social worker" help the client come up with a self-instruction script in order to be better able to face a challenging situation.

Thought-Stopping Techniques

Sometimes, even after people have learned that certain thought patterns they have are distorted, they still have difficulty putting a stop to those thoughts. To interrupt or stop negative thoughts, three techniques can be taught:

- thought-stopping
- the rubber-band technique
- setting aside worry time

1. *Thought stopping.* When alone and thinking negatively, clients are instructed to yell "STOP" as loudly as possible and to then say, "I won't think about that anymore." They are told to gradually change from yelling to thinking "Stop" so the technique can be used in public.

EXAMPLE 6-3

Cheryl, an African American 18-year-old, has been living with a foster family, Mr. and Mrs. Johnson, for the last 2 years. Also in the household is the Johnson's biological grandchild, Kenny, of whom they have custody. Since Cheryl has graduated from high school, her foster parents expect her to get a job, but she has not been looking. Cheryl is also not doing her chores or complying with the Johnsons' house rules. After the social work student worked with Cheryl, Cheryl better understood the connection between the way she thought ("They're going to kick me out"), the way she felt (anger at them), and the way she behaved (wanting to get back at them and not get a job). Cheryl had also figured out that, "Being kicked out is just what I'm used to from my past foster parents. My real mom—that's what she did, too. She kicked me out of the house when I was really young." Then she said, "I just don't know how to stop having these thoughts that they don't love me and that they want me to leave."

   The intern introduced the technique of *thought-stopping* to Cheryl and explained that every time she thought about the Johnsons kicking her out or not loving her, or had any other negative thought that was not realistic or based on facts or evidence, she should use the technique. They practiced in the session with Cheryl first saying "Stop!" very loudly when she had the negative thoughts and then saying it to herself.

2. *The rubber-band technique.* In this technique, clients are told to wear a rubber band on their wrist and snap it every time they catch themselves thinking negatively.

3. *Setting aside worry time.* For people who are beset with rumination about negative and disastrous events, this technique can be helpful in introducing an element of control over the worry. It involves scheduling a preset time each day to focus on troubling issues. The idea is to make an appointment with oneself for worrying; 15 minutes should be plenty. For this technique, the person is encouraged to write down his or her concerns; the act of writing itself often makes endless rumination more concrete and manageable.

EXAMPLE 6-4

A 24-year-old Caucasian woman named Margie talked with a social worker about feeling fat, ugly, depressed, and worried that everyone was thinking these things about her. She said she also worried about what was going to happen in her life. She still hadn't finished college, and she had no career plan. She didn't have a boyfriend, and she worried that she would never get one. She ruminated constantly about her last relationship in which a man she'd been seeing abruptly stopped calling. Finally, she worried about her father, with whom she lived, because if she moved out eventually, he would be lonely (his wife, Margie's mother, had divorced him), even though Margie had no immediate plans to move out.

The social worker gave her the homework assignment of "worry time" because Margie said these thoughts consumed her during the day. She recognized that they also blocked her from taking more productive actions, such as finding a job and getting involved with activities and volunteer work that might lead to meeting new people or finding a career path.

Margie religiously stuck to the assignment for the first week and said that it was enormously helpful. She was able to tell herself during the day when worries surfaced, "I can think about that later during worry time." She said when she sat down to worry, it was harder than she thought (sometimes she wouldn't feel like worrying then), but the writing kept her on track.

During the second week, Margie said that she didn't need to use so much worry time unless she found herself worrying during the day. Then she would tell herself, "I won't let that bother me now. I can think about this later during worry time." Margie had started filling out applications and going on job interviews. She was also planning more activities with friends, such as rollerblading, and was more focused on enjoying herself than on thinking about how ugly and fat she was.

Exercise 6-5

Consider a negative or distorted thought pattern you frequently experience that you would like to gain control over (we all have them!). Choose one of the above thought-stopping techniques and try it for one day with the negative thought pattern. Give the reason you chose the particular technique and the results of your experiment. From your practice with the technique, how will you help clients use the technique?

Coping with Craving

Craving is commonly associated with substance use but can also apply to other situations, such as when people are trying to break up with abusive or inappropriate partners. Sometimes people return to using substances or go back with abusive or inappropriate partners because they experience over-whelming feelings of craving or longing and give in to them (Carroll, 1998). However, if this common phenomenon is understood and anticipated, then these feelings can be managed effectively. Although craving has certain physi-ological components, mostly it is a psychological experience. We describe both cognitive and behavioral ways to manage craving.

Cues for the craving first need to be identified. Cues for craving the return of an old relationship, for example, might include certain times of the day (e.g., going to bed alone at night), experiencing a setback in a new lifestyle, feeling lonely, or seeing other couples together. Craving for substance use can occur in reaction to a variety of triggers, including emotions (e.g., boredom), social cues (being with people who use substances), and environment (being in the neighborhood where one used to use substances or where drugs are avail-able). The social worker's task is to help the client identify these cues and to convey the time-limited nature of longing, that it peaks and dissipates, if not acted upon. After identifying the person's most problematic cues, the social worker should explore the degree to which of some of these can be avoided— for example, keeping busy with a structured list if being bored is a challenge, avoiding places where a certain person might be.

The variety of strategies for coping with craving include the following: distraction; talking about craving; "going with" the craving; recalling the negative consequences of the object of craving; and using self-talk (Carroll, 1998). Distraction involves keeping busy and engaging in enjoyable and relax-ing activities. Talking about the craving involves conversing with supportive people about the feelings. In "going with the craving," Carroll describes the following: "The idea behind this technique is to let cravings occur, peak, and pass; in other words, to experience them without fighting or giving in to them." Ito and colleagues as cited in Carroll (1998) identified the steps involved; these should be practiced within sessions or at home before craving occurs. Also, clients should be told that the purpose is not to make the cravings disappear, but to experience them in a different way that makes them less anxiety provoking and dangerous and thus easier to ride out. The steps are as follows:

1. Find someplace safe to let oneself experience craving (e.g., a comfortable and quiet place at home).
2. Relax and focus on the experience of craving itself—where it occurs in the body or mind and how intense it is.
3. Focus on the area where the craving occurs. This involves paying attention to all the somatic and affective signals and trying to put them into words. What is the feeling like? Where is it? How strong is it? Does it move or change? Where else does it occur?

Another technique to assist clients in resisting craving involves recalling the negative consequences of the problem behavior. When experiencing craving, many people have a tendency to remember only positive aspects, often forgetting the negative consequences. For this reason, one recommendation is that a client carry an index card with the positives of staying away from the problem behavior and the negative consequences of giving in to it written out (see also the discussion on the decisional balance technique in Chapter 9).

Self-talk may also be a strategy to use. Automatic thoughts associated with craving often have a sense of urgency and exaggerated dire consequences (e.g., "If I don't see him tonight, I'll die.") In coping with craving, the client needs to both recognize the automatic thoughts and counter them effectively. To help clients recognize their automatic thoughts, you can point out cognitive distortions that occur during sessions (e.g., "A few times today you've said you need to talk to her, see how she's doing. Are you aware of those thoughts when you have them?"). Another strategy is to help clients "slow down the tape" to recognize cognitions: "When you relapsed last time, you said you really weren't aware of what led up to it. But I bet if we go back and try to remember what that day was like, sort of play it back like a movie in slow motion, we could find a couple of examples of things you said to yourself, maybe without even realizing it, that led you down that path. Can you sort of play last night back for us now?"

Once automatic thoughts are identified, it becomes much easier to counter or confront them, using positive rather than negative self-talk. This includes cognitions such as challenging the thought (e.g., "I won't really die if I don't have her in my life"), and normalizing the feeling (e.g., "Craving is uncomfortable, but a lot of people have it and it's something I can deal with without using").

EXAMPLE 6-5

John, a 36-year-old habitual marijuana and alcohol user, was arrested for driving while intoxicated. The court mandated that he attend treatment and undergo periodic urinalysis as part of his sentencing. John was divorced, with no children, and currently lived alone. John expressed to the social worker providing his treatment that he had overwhelming urges to use marijuana. Together they devised a plan for how he would cope with these cravings. First, they looked at the cues for his craving. John initially said he felt like he didn't have cues—he just craved marijuana constantly. The social worker attempted to walk him through his day to get more infor- mation. John said he'd usually started smoking first thing in the morning when he got up. He also was usually "high" when he went to his job. He was a television repairman and claimed that being high helped him focus on this work, which required concentration but was also tedious. Lunchtime was another time of day that initiated cravings because then he had usually smoked another "joint" before returning to his afternoon shift of work. Coming home marked another occasion, since he was used to "lighting one up" right when he entered his rental house. Weekends were another problem, because he went to bars with his friends and got high several times on weekends.

Given this information, the social worker identified that "certain times of day" were John's major cue. Because he had a 15-year-old entrenched routine with his marijuana use, she advised that the best strategy was to use a form of distraction coupled with avoidance, which meant changing his routines.

For instance, she asked him if he had other morning routines he enjoyed. He said he liked drinking coffee and in the past, would smoke, watch TV, and drink a pot of coffee before heading to work. After some deliberation, they decided that John could try visiting a place that sold "really good coffee" in the morning and drink his coffee there. He balked at the expense, but when the social worker pointed out that spending money on coffee was a lot less expensive than maintaining a marijuana habit, he had to laugh at himself.

For lunchtime, they talked about John treating himself to lunch out rather than going home to smoke. The social worker also informed him about lunchtime A.A. meetings that were quite common throughout the city and where he could safely talk about his cravings. So far, John had balked at A.A. attendance, but he admitted he might have to do something to meet people who didn't smoke because he didn't know a single person outside of that network. John said he also enjoyed browsing in computer and record stores, so this was another pleasurable activity he could do on his lunch hour to replace marijuana smoking.

In this fashion, they went through his daily and weekend routines, trying to find alternative ways of meeting some of his needs for relaxation and pleasure. In addition, the social worker reminded him that in the early phase of treatment, they had done a decisional balance on the advantages and disadvantages of changing his behavior. She suggested that he carry a copy of it folded in his wallet, so when he was beset with cravings, he could remember the negative consequences of his use. Major ones for him involved the legal trouble he was in, the fact that he was more than 50 pounds overweight from drinking and the "munchies" that followed his marijuana use, and a chronic cough that had afflicted him for years. He also recognized that his ex-wife had left him because of his substance use in the past, and to be involved with a partner in the future, he was going to have to "straighten up." He didn't want to live alone for the rest of his life.

Self-talk was another strategy they explored. John identified his thoughts as: "I don't think I can get through the day without smoking." Response: "That is not true. I've gotten through plenty of days without smoking." "Marijuana was the best thing in my life." Response: "The best thing in my life has made me overweight and unhealthy and means that I now have a record."

Exercise 6-6

Do you have cravings associated with a particular problem (say, overeating or smoking)? Choose one of the methods to cope with one incident of your craving and report the results here. What have you learned that you can apply to your work with clients?

Exercise 6-7

Do you have a client on your caseload who experiences cravings, whether for an abusive partner or for drugs or alcohol? Do one of the following. (a) Work directly with the client on understanding the nature of cravings; then explain and practice at least one technique for dealing with craving. (b) Work hypothetically with a partner in class on this exercise. Summarize the work in a paragraph and then report what you have learned about this type of work.

Summary

This chapter focused on helping clients learn coping skills that are cognitive in nature. These skills are needed when people have certain deficits in their thinking. Self-talk, self-instruction, thought-stopping, and positive ways to cope with craving require the client to develop new cognitions to assist them in managing and negotiating stressful events more effectively.

References

Carroll, K. (1998). *A cognitive-behavioral approach: Treating cocaine addiction.* Online http://www.drugabuse.gov/TXManuals/CBT/CBT1.html. Accessed February 3, 2005.

Meichenbaum, D., & Deffenbacher, J. (1988). Stress inoculation training. *Counseling Psychologist, 16,* 69–90.

Spence, S. (1994). Practitioner review: Cognitive therapy with children and adolescents. *Journal of Child Psychology and Psychiatry, 35,* 1191–1228.

Spiegler, M. (1993). *Contemporary behavior therapy,* 2nd ed. Belmont, CA: Brooks/Cole.

7

— ▼▲▼ —

Behaviorally Based Skills

This chapter focuses on the repertoire of skills the social worker can teach the client. These include the following: problem-solving, relaxation, communication, assertiveness, and social skills. Although the skills are discussed separately, cognitive-behavioral interventions are often offered as a package, and many techniques are used in combination. The chapter concludes with how the various techniques can be used to develop a plan for coping.

Problem-Solving Training

Individuals often get stuck when faced with stressful situations, not knowing what to do about them. They may avoid the problem altogether. For instance, a woman receives a letter from the electric company stating that her electricity will be turned off for nonpayment. Unable to face the problem, she does nothing. Another common way that people deal with stressful situations is to use a tactic that has not worked well before. For example, a child misbehaves, and the parent yells, even though yelling has proven in the past to have no effect on the child.

The problem-solving process is designed to help clients learn how to produce a variety of potentially effective responses when faced with problem situations (D'Zurilla & Nezu, 2001). It includes the following five steps for the practitioner and client to address:

1. Define the problem.
2. Brainstorm.
3. Evaluate the alternatives.
4. Choose and implement an alternative.
5. Evaluate the implemented option.

We flesh out the steps, drawing on material from Beach, Sandeen, and O'Leary (1990), D'Zurilla and Nezu (2001), and Wheeler, Christensen, and Jacobson (2001). A Problem-Solving Process worksheet is provided for your use.

Defining the problem involves first finding the salient problem. For instance, a client mentions that she is often late for work, but then mentions the reason for her lateness: her children not getting ready on time. The latter should therefore be the focus of the problem-solving process.

Defining the problem may also mean breaking a complex problem into its subcomponents. For instance, if a couple's finances are in a tangle, this problem may have to be tackled one part at a time. The couple could spend time on one aspect, such as figuring out how to spend 20 percent less each month. Note how the problems should be defined in concrete terms, such as "spending 20 percent less each month." Although some goals are not easily defined in terms of their positive behaviors, the focus, as much as possible, should be on what people want rather than on what they don't want. For example, it could be "how to discuss finances calmly" rather than "how to not argue over money."

Brainstorming is the part of the problem-solving process in which the client is encouraged to come up with as many solutions as possible—even those that are silly, outlandish, or impossible. If more than one person is taking part in the process, the social worker should ensure gaining feedback from everyone. One way to do this in a particularly unruly group or one in which there are dominating members is to ask each person in turn for an idea and keep going around the room until a sufficient number of ideas have been presented.

WORKSHEET 7–1 **Problem-Solving Process**

Defining the Problem

Brainstorming
1.
2.
3.
4.
5.
6.
7.
8.
9.
10.

WORKSHEET 7–1 (*continued*)

Evaluating the Alternatives
1. Advantages/Disadvantages
2. Advantages/Disadvantages
3. Advantages/Disadvantages
Choosing and Implementing an Alternative
Evaluating the Implemented Option

Sometimes it is only after people come up with a number of ideas that they become "warmed up" and consider other options. Some prompts to get ideas going include the following:

- What would [an important person in a family member's life] say you might do about this?
- What would [people family members admire] do in this situation?
- Think about what you have done to solve other problems like this in the past.
- "Ask questions that prompt different classes of solutions (e.g., 'Are there any consequences that might help Johnny clean his room?' 'Try thinking of some ways to change your routine that might help you . . .'") (Foster & Robin, 1998, p. 636).
- Make an off-the-wall or "crazy" suggestion yourself.

All solutions should be written down.

Sometimes clients at this stage will attempt to dismiss certain ideas or argue about their feasibility; however, the social worker should redirect the brainstorming process, stating that the time for evaluating alternatives will come later. When people criticize, they should be asked to come up with a solution instead.

When **evaluating alternatives**, the patently irrelevant or impossible items are crossed out before each viable alternative is examined for its advantages and disadvantages. Sometimes in this process, clients find that they need to collect more information. For example, the couple with financial problems might need to find out more information about credit consolidation programs or credit counseling options.

The next part of the problem-solving process is **choosing and implementing an alternative** in which the social worker has the client select one or more strategies that seem to maximize benefits over costs. The details of the plan may need to be fleshed out in writing. As part of the plan, potential barriers should be identified. Practice of skills may also be necessary. As a final aspect, the social worker should elicit a commitment from the client to follow through with the plan.

Evaluating the implemented option involves exploring with the client how the plan was enacted and its subsequent effect. Praise is used liberally for the elements of the plan that went well as well. The social worker also spends time on the parts of the plan that may still need work. If necessary, the plan is revised or a new option is selected from the list.

EXAMPLE 7-1

In a group designed to enhance coping skills with adolescent girls, one of the units covered problem-solving. The teen girls, who were attending an after-school pregnancy prevention program, wanted to discuss how to handle unwanted attention from males, a problem that seemed to come up on a frequent basis.

The members generated a list of possible options. These included the following:

1. saying "no thanks"
2. saying "leave me alone" or "go away"
3. laughing it off/joking around
4. ignoring/walking away
5. speaking to a parent about it
6. making excuses, such as "I have a boyfriend"
7. using "the finger" and/or other expletives

The advantage of the more aggressive options was that they "did work." Girls said they were able to get boys (and men) to leave them alone by using these means. However, they said a main disadvantage was they didn't feel good about themselves for using these methods. Another was that they wouldn't feel safe doing these things alone—only when they were in a group of other girls. Options that involved "trying to be nice," such as saying "no thanks" or "leave me alone," laughing off an advance, or ignoring someone that was being sexually aggressive, were also discussed. The main advantage of these methods was that they were effective; the disadvantage was that sometimes males did not take them seriously. Regarding the option of speaking to a parent, the advantage was that girls could receive advice from parents about how to handle a situation they found difficult; the disadvantage was that their freedom might be at cost as their mothers might not let them go to as many places. The other alternative explored was "making excuses." While this was advantageous in that it "sometimes worked," for many sexually aggressive males, excuses didn't seem to have much of a deterrent effect. Group members discussed the various options and determined that it helped to be assertive by telling people who "came on to them" to leave them alone. If that didn't work, they thought that ignoring further advances was the best course of action.

The problem-solving process is taught not only to people on an individual basis, but also to couples and families. It is sometimes then referred to as "negotiation skills." Some additional challenges may arise when problem-solving is presented in a family context (Foster & Robin, 1998). First, family members may believe that the problem-solving process seems "fake." The social worker can explain that many new skills seem artificial at first. After the family becomes more adept at the skill, they can adapt it to suit its members. Sometimes people complain that by focusing on a specific problem, the "real problem" is being ignored. The social worker must explain that problems manifest themselves in specific ways, and it is only by naming concrete behaviors that people understand the nature of a problem and what it is they must do to change their behavior. Family members also may complain that their problems are too complex for problem-solving techniques. In these situations, the social worker should break large, complex problems into their constituent parts and work on one at a time.

Another common problem in conjoint sessions is that certain family members exert more power than others, and they either force others to accept their definition of the problem, or they dominate the brainstorming, evaluation, or selection phases. The social worker must reassure the family that all members have the right to be heard and understood and that sometimes different definitions of the problem are necessary so that the problem is illuminated more fully. The social worker should ask everyone in the room to give brainstorming ideas. If it appears that people are afraid of offering opinions that are in conflict to a dominant member, the social worker must bring this out into the open. For resistant, sullen, or passive members, ask them to assume roles that involve participation in the process, such as writing down solutions and reading them back, or writing down the pros and cons of viable alternatives.

To make sure that positions are understood, for those on "opposite sides," say each partner in a couple or the children and the parents in a family, have each party evaluate the advantages and disadvantages of each viable solution from the other party's perspective. If parties come to an impasse on a certain solution—one side wants one idea implemented and the other side wants another— ask the couple or the family to implement one solution one week (usually the children's), and if it doesn't work, to try the next idea the following week.

Exercise 7-1

Consider a problem with which you are struggling. Go through the problem-solving process. If you are comfortable sharing your problem with a classmate, have this person go through the process with you. As you come to the end of the process, decide what options you will implement in order to help solve your problem.

Exercise 7-2

This exercise is best done as a class. Have a student in the class volunteer a problem in his or her field placement or a challenge he or she is having with a particular case. Go through the problem-solving process as a class. Aside from the answers to the particular dilemma involved with the student, what did you learn about the problem-solving process? How can you apply what you have learned to your work with clients?

Exercise 7-3

Consider a problem with which a client is struggling. It could be financial, a transportation issue, or how to handle a situation at work or with family. Go through the problem-solving process using worksheet 1 with a classmate as part of a role-play situation.

Relaxation Training

The purpose of training people in relaxation skills is to help them reduce their anxiety and tension. Techniques for relaxation training include diaphragmatic breathing, progressive muscle relaxation, meditation, and visualization (described in this section and discussed more extensively in Davis, Eshelman, & McKay, 1995). When people are trained in these skills, they are instructed to practice them daily, for at least 10 to 15 minutes per day. Relaxation training can also be considered more broadly as any activity that reduces tension and induces a feeling of well-being in a client. "Self-care" activities in general can be counted in this category. Clients often name a number of such activities that are pleasant and enjoyable, such as gardening, craftmaking, talking on the phone to friends, going out to eat and hot baths or showers.

The purpose of *diaphragmatic breathing*, which involves deep breathing into the abdomen, is to reduce muscle tension and to increase functioning of the respiratory system. Diaphragmatic breathing, in contrast to people's common pattern of breathing through the chest, prevents rapid, shallow breathing and hyperventilation associated with anxiety.

In *progressive muscle relaxation*, the individual is instructed to tense the muscles in his or her arms and hands, then relax them (Clark, Lewinsohn, & Hops, 1990). Next the individual is asked to tense his or her face and forehead, followed by the shoulders, back, chest, and stomach, then legs. After tensing each muscle group, the person is told to relax and is given instructions about abdominal breathing and the effect of breathing deeply on relaxation. Approximately 7 seconds are devoted to tensing each muscle group and 7 seconds are devoted to relaxing the same muscle group.

The process of *meditation* involves the uncritical focus of attention in order to gain detachment from troublesome thoughts and emotions. It also helps the person to concentrate more fully on the present moment rather than on the past or future. The focus of attention varies by tradition but can include the person's own breathing; a word or phrase; the visualization of an object, such as a flame or a flower; or gazing at a fixed object, such as a lit candle. The position used during meditation also varies by tradition but can include sitting in a straight-backed chair, sitting cross-legged, or holding a yoga position.

Visualization involves creating a special image or place that is relaxing and using the five senses to conjure up details of the experience. More discussion of techniques can be found in the self-help books on relaxation that are listed in the appendix.

The following case involves Monisha Jackson, whom we discussed in Chapter 4, Example 4–1.

EXAMPLE 7-2

Ms. Jackson, the mother of two children with sickle cell anemia, suffered much stress and anxiety and did not have many ways to reduce tension. When the social work brought up visualization, Ms. Jackson said she'd heard of the technique before: "I think that's what a psychologist once taught my youngest daughter to do when she was in pain. Some kind of storytelling or something. You can tell me more about it."

The social work intern asked Ms. Jackson to identify a place that was relaxing for her (a Caribbean beach), and the intern wrote down the sensory (sight, smell, auditory, tactile) details that Ms. Jackson used to describe the place. The intern told her that in times of anxiety or stress, Ms. Jackson could sit in a relaxing position, close her eyes, and conjure up the place and experience these details. They practiced in the session, and Ms. Jackson reported feeling a sense of relaxation and being renewed.

Exercise 7-4

What are your self-care activities?

Exercise 7-5

What is your experience with relaxation training and visualization?

Exercise 7-6

Talk with a client whom you think might benefit from self-care activities. Proceed into relaxation training or visualization if the client seems like he or she could benefit and is receptive. If you did this training, report on the client response and what you learned about this technique.

Communication Skills Training

Communication skills cover a wide spectrum of interventions that includes attention to clients' assertiveness and social skills (which will be covered later in the chapter) as well as negotiation skills. This section explores communication skills in light of situations social workers commonly encounter. These include fostering healthy communication in families in which stressful life events have occurred and helping clients advocate for themselves in written communication.

The reasons for facilitating clients' communication skills are myriad. Positive communication builds relationships and closeness with others, which in turn enhances social support (Clark, Lewinsohn, & Hops, 1990). Social support not only provides a source of positive reinforcement, but also buffers individuals from stressful life events. In addition, processing the effects of problems with other people may change a person's perspective on problem-generating events. When a person can openly state feelings and reactions to interpersonal situations, other people understand clearly how they might continue their positive behaviors or change their negative behavior.

The basic components of communication skills training include using "I" messages, reflective and empathic listening, making clear behavior change requests, and complimenting. "I" messages are those in which a person talks about his or her own position and feelings in a situation rather than making accusatory comments about another person. The general format for giving "I" messages is *I feel (the reaction) to what happened (a specific activating event)*. For example, "I feel worried when you stay out past curfew on Saturday night" rather than "How dare you stay out so late!" which may make the other person feel defensive.

Since people have a tendency to offer opinions instead of expressing their feelings (e.g., "I feel that you have been neglecting me"), the social worker is advised to educate clients about the four main feelings: anger, sadness, fear, and happiness. When clients have difficulty talking about their feelings, they can refer to these emotions to keep them on track (e.g., "I feel sad that you haven't called me from work recently to talk during the day").

A good guideline for when to initiate the use of "I" messages is when people are interested in working on a relationship or when they need someone to change his or her behavior because that person can't be avoided (Clark, Lewinsohn, & Hops, 1990). If a person can be easily avoided, then it might not be worth doing the work and taking the risk involved in making "I" messages.

Listening skills include both reflective listening and validation of the other person's intent. The purpose of reflective listening is to ensure that the listener understands the speaker's perspective. It decreases the tendency of people to draw premature conclusions about the intentions and meaning of another's statement (Cordova & Jacobson, 1993).

Reflective listening involves paraphrasing back the feelings and content of the speaker's message with the format "What I hear you saying is . . ." or "You seem to feel [mad, sad, scared, and happy] when . . ." Beyond reflection, validation is an advanced skill and involves conveying that, given the other person's perspectives and assumptions, his or her experiences are legitimate and understandable: "I can see that if you were thinking I had done that, you would feel that way" (Beach, Sandeen, & O'Leary, 1990).

A third component of communication skills training involves teaching people to make clear behavior requests of others. Such requests should always be

- Specific ("pick up your toys") rather than global ("clean up around here").
- Measurable ("I would like you to call once a day").
- Stated as the presence of positive behaviors rather than the absence of negative behaviors ("Give me a chance to change and look over the mail when I come home, and then I'll talk to you" rather than "stop bothering me with your questions").

Praising or complimenting is also considered an essential communication skill because it reinforces desired behaviors in others so that they will continue to occur. (See Chapter 2 for information on praise.) Another purpose is to create a positive atmosphere in the relationship so that other interventions will be more effective when they are applied.

While communication skills seem fairly straightforward when they are laid out in this way, people typically have enormous difficulty learning these skills. Table 7–1 covers some of the common challenges with ways you, as the social worker, can respond. To help you get in touch with some of these possible difficulties yourself, a couple of exercises follow for you to try out your own skills.

Exercise 7-7

Consider a difficult interaction in your personal or professional life (e.g., handling a disagreement with a family member or friend, talking to your field instructor about your learning needs, addressing a group member for a class project about contributing more to the group). Rate from 1 to 10 how comfortable you are communicating about this issue. Go through the Communication Skills Training worksheet, giving thought to and then writing down how you would handle the various aspects of communication that might be involved in this situation. After you have finished, rate from 1 to 10 how comfortable you are now in communicating about this issue.

TABLE 7–1 Challenges in Learning Communication Skills

Challenges	How to Help
People use "I" messages that are really disguised "you" messages (e.g., "I feel like you never listen to me").	Remind people to talk about their feelings first (e.g., "I feel sad when . . .").
People make global statements about the other person rather than describing specific behaviors (e.g., "You never listen to me").	Remind people to describe specific behaviors (e.g., "I tell you about my day, and you keep watching TV").
People are hesitant to do reflective listening because they think that by reflecting another's feelings they are agreeing with the other person's version of events.	Reassure people that they don't have to agree with what the other person is saying; they just have to reflect back the content of the message (e.g., "You're saying that you feel sad when you tell me about your day, and I'm watching TV"). Tell them that they will have a chance to state their side of the to situation.
People ask for change from the other person that is stated in global terms (e.g., "If you could just be nice to me").	Indicate that change requests should be made as specific behaviors (e.g., "I would like you to turn off the TV when I'm telling you about my day").
People say that they shouldn't have to ask for what they want— the other person should already know.	Remind people that others are not "mind-readers" and that we all find different things important, so the other person must be told what we consider important.
People are reluctant to praise others for the behaviors they want ("He should already be doing these things. He never says anything nice to me, so why should I say anything nice to him?").	Let people know that praise is important because it lets others know they are on track in giving us what we would like. Praise is also a reciprocal process, and positive feelings engendered by praise may lead to the other person offering praise in turn.

WORKSHEET 7–2 Communication Skills Training

Skill	Example
"I" messages	
Reflective listening	
Validation	
Making behavior requests of others	
Giving praise/compliments	

Exercise 7-8

Now for the more advanced exercise. Take your work from the previous exercise and implement it with the person involved. Write the responses you received to each of the communication skills you tried. What is your overall assessment of how the interaction went? Did you get what you wanted?

Exercise 7-9

Teach a client about "I" messages, reflective listening, and making behavior change requests. Before initiating the training, have the client rate on a scale of 1 to 10 his or her comfort level in dealing with the particular interaction involved. Anchor 10 as being "absolutely comfortable" and 1 as being "extremely uncomfortable." Record the client's reactions to the skills, noting what represented a challenge. Did you make any adaptations to meet the needs of this client? After you have finished the training, re-rate his or her comfort level.

Communication skills can be taught to people on an individual basis or in couple or family sessions. When people are taught these skills in conjoint sessions, expect that they have an even more difficult time grasping the information and rehearsing it. Often, family members become defensive or argumentative; they interrupt each other and attempt to control the session (Foster & Robin, 1998). In this situation, the social worker should establish ground rules, such as one person talks at a time and there will be no interrupting each other; when ground rules are transgressed, the social worker then has the rule to refer back to. Politely but firmly redirecting family members to the task at hand, rather than allowing interruptions and angry outbursts to take over the session, may be necessary. In some cases, when family members do not respond to redirection and quarrels overrun the session, the social worker may have to work with family members on anger management skills. Working with family members separately until they have the skills to control their anger and express themselves in appropriate ways in session is sometimes necessary.

Exercise 7-10

If you are working with a couple or with a family, teach the basic communication skills of "I" messages, reflective listening, and making behavior requests. What were their reactions to these skills? Did anyone argue or interrupt, or were there other challenges for you to manage? How did you handle them? Write out the gist of the messages family members were eventually able to give each other.

Another way that social workers can use communication skills training is when they work with families in which there are a multitude of stressors. Often, our clients are undergoing chronic stress, such as poverty, living in unsafe neighborhoods, abuse, and living in single-parent homes. They also experience acute stressors, such as divorce and remarriage, moving residences, illness of a caregiver or relative, and so forth. Children under stress may act out in externalizing ways, and parents are often puzzled by their children's behavior, asking social workers to work with their children on reducing these symptoms. Children may also of course react in internalizing ways with anxiety, depression, and low self-esteem, which might be less manifest to the parent.

Social workers can teach parents in these situations about the effects of stress on children and assist them in identifying their children's feelings and in responding appropriately with reflective listening. Training parents in such skills is necessary so that they can help their children deal with the impact of stress as it unfolds.

However, parents sometimes are reluctant to talk with their children about what they have been through. Following are some of the typical remarks parents make and how the social worker may respond (adapted from Deblinger & Heflin, 1996):

> *Parent:* I don't want to talk about what has happened or what is happening with my child. I just want him to forget about it.
>
> *Social Worker Response:*
> - Discuss the research indicating that avoidance is a poor coping mechanism and leads to less than optimal outcomes (Compas et al., 2001).
> - Provide the rationale that important behavior is modeled when a parent is able to talk about family experiences and identify feelings; the child learns how to communicate about experiences and feelings rather than acting them out through behaviors.
> - Just because something is forbidden from discussion doesn't mean that a child won't continue to mull things over and possibly reach erroneous conclusions about what has happened ("it's my fault").

Parent: I'd rather you just talked to my child and got through to him.

Social Work Response:

- Stress to parents that they are much more important to their child than the social worker will ever be. Children often take awhile to reveal experiences and feelings, and the social worker may have a limited time to work with a child.
- If parents are trained in some important listening and validation skills, then they can help their children with experiences and reactions as they unfold over time.

Parent: What if I get upset?

Social Work Response:

- The parent can process the events and experiences with the social worker first so that emotions are expressed before talking with the child.
- The social worker can provide guidance to help parents, when they become upset, to reassure their children that the children are not to blame for the parents' feelings.
- Parents are also advised to express their feelings to their children ("I am feeling sad that your dad and I are no longer going to be living together") so that children learn how to identify and articulate feelings.
- Parents can further reassure children that they have other adults to turn to for support, and these people should be named. In this way, children realize that they are not responsible for taking care of their parents.

Parent: What if my child gets upset?

Social Work Response:

- The social worker can advise parents that they should see this as a positive sign that their children are expressing their feelings, and the child should be reinforced ("I'm glad you told me about this").
- Parents can reflectively listen to the child's concerns and offer comfort.

Parent: I won't know what to say. I can't explain to her why some of these things have happened.

Social Worker Response:

- Reflectively listen to children's concerns.
- Admit that aspects of what has happened are difficult to understand (e.g., death of a loved one).
- Have the parent tell the child that he or she will seek guidance from the social worker.

Parent: The only time my child is interested in talking is when I'm busy.

Social Work Response:

- Take time out to listen to children's concerns, if possible.
- If not possible, assure your child that you will come back to the topic later and set a specific time to do so.

Exercise 7-11

If you are working with a parent who has concerns about his or her child's behavior and the family has undergone stressors, teach the parent about the use of reflective listening and validation of children's experiences and feelings. Did the parent respond in any of the ways described in this section? How did you handle any reluctance the parent had? Ask the parent, after your training is complete, to report back the results of such a conversation with his or her child. What happened?

As an alternative, if you do not have a client who would benefit from this exercise, role play such a client with a classmate and go through the same steps.

Another way that clients can learn about communication is by expressing themselves in writing as part of advocating for themselves. For those situations in which verbal communication skills have not been sufficient to result in a desired outcome, the social worker might focus, as the next step, on helping the client compose a letter to the agency or organization that handles the client's particular matter. Such a letter usually records the actions the client has taken to date. In this way, clients learn to be behaviorally specific about what they have done, referring to the policies that entitle them services, and they make concrete requests about the next step that the other party should take. Teaching communication skills through letter-writing is an effective way to help clients learn about their rights and how to have these rights met.

Exercise 7-12

Find a client on your own caseload or at your agency whose rights have been violated in some way (not being treated fairly by an employer, not receiving services for a child, not having basic living requirements met by the place in which they are housed). Meet with the particular client, review any records he or she has of previous requests or actions, and help the client compose a letter detailing the past events and the corrective action that must be taken. Make sure the letter gets sent. It might take awhile to obtain results, but please discuss with your class the results of your actions.

Assertiveness Skills

Assertiveness training involves teaching people to communicate their rights to others. Such training involves first teaching the difference between aggression (putting forth one's opinions, feelings, and needs at the expense of others), assertion (expressing one's needs with respect for the rights of others), and passivity (putting other people's needs over one's own) (Davis, Eshelman, & McKay, 1995). The second aspect of training involves identifying the different situations in which people typically have difficulty demonstrating assertiveness. These include

- asking for help or service
- stating a difference of opinion
- receiving and expressing negative or positive feelings
- asking for cooperation
- speaking up about something that is annoying
- talking when he or she is at the center of attention

The assessment also involves identifying the particular people with whom the client acts nonassertively. These may include parents, children, colleagues, spouse, partner, employer, acquaintances, strangers, friends, salespeople, clerks, and/or a group of more than two or three people.

Once the situations have been identified, assertiveness skills training includes some basic communication skills, such as teaching the client to use "I" statements and make behavior change requests to get his or her needs met in a way that is respectful of others. Other assertiveness skills include the "broken record technique" in which a person repeats his or her position without continuing to argue a particular point. More discussion of techniques can be found in the self-help books on assertiveness that are listed in the appendix.

EXAMPLE 7-3

In a group of mothers whose children had been sexually abused, assertiveness was one of the group topics. Women went through a list of situations and identified those that gave them problems, including setting limits with the person who abused their child. For instance, one group member named Martha described how her ex-boyfriend, who had sexually abused her 9-year-old daughter, kept calling and coming over even though she was at risk of losing custody of her child if he had contact with her.

The group facilitators modeled how to handle the situation, using "I" messages and behavior change requests: "I'm mad that even after I've told you that I can't see you or talk to you, you keep contacting me. I've told you that I need to put my daughter first, and you ignore what I say. I don't want you calling or coming over anymore."

Martha said that the problem was he would start to deny the abuse, taking her daughter's allegations, one by one, and refuting them. She said she wanted to be fair and hear both sides of the story but admitted that listening to what he had to say made her feel confused and that her daughter probably didn't feel supported as a result. The facilitators discussed the "broken record" technique as it related to Martha's situation. They explained that rather than getting "sucked into" debating with him her daughter's allegations, she could simply repeat her request: "I have to put my daughter first right now, and I don't want you calling or coming over." After she behaviorally rehearsed the dialogue with one of the facilitators, Martha said that even though she was nervous using these skills, she felt more confident that she could actually set limits on her ex-boyfriend.

Exercise 7-13

Assess your own assertiveness skills on a 1-to-10 scale, with 1 being passive, 10 being aggressive, and 5 being assertive. Identify a situation in which you have difficulty being assertive and write down the responses you could make that would put you in the assertive range on the scale. How confident are you on a 1-to-10 scale that you can enact this skill the next time the situation arises?

For the next part of this exercise, role play your new assertive response with a classmate. Rate again your confidence on a 1-to-10 scale.

Exercise 7-14

Working with a client who needs help with assertiveness skills, ask the person to assess his or her own assertiveness skills on a 1-to-10 scale, with 1 being passive, 10 being aggressive, and 5 being assertive. Have the person identify a situation in which he or she has difficulty being assertive, and teach assertiveness skills. Model the appropriate response, and then have the person behaviorally rehearse. Have the person rate on a 1-to-10 scale his or her sense of confidence that the skill will be enacted the next time the situation arises. What barriers are still in the way? What do you need to help the person overcome these barriers? Write down a summary of this work.

As an alternative, if you do not have a client who might benefit from assertiveness skills, role play such a client with a classmate and proceed through the steps above.

Social Skills Training

When people are taught social skills, they are more successful at eliciting positive reinforcement from their environments. Such skills lead to more positive interactions and help build or improve relationships. The most basic skills involve making eye contact, smiling at least once or more when in conversation with another person, saying something positive about the other person, and revealing some personal information ("I usually take the earlier bus"). When teaching social skills, the social worker should model these behaviors and then allow the client to rehearse.

The next skill that is addressed is when to start a conversation and what to say. People are told that good times to start conversations are when the other person makes eye contact, when the other person says "hello," and when in a common situation (waiting for a bus or in a line). They are also taught to avoid starting conversations when another person looks busy, preoccupied, or angry. Examples of conversational topics are recommended: weather, sports, or anything else that the individual might share in common with the other person. Finally, clients are given instruction in how to leave a conversation. In a large group, they can just say, "excuse me" and leave with a smile. In smaller groups of two to three people, they are given suggestions, such as "I think I'll go get something to eat" or "I'd like to talk to so-and-so over there. I'll see you later."

EXAMPLE 7–4

Evelyn was a 19-year-old Hispanic female who came to the United States from El Salvador a year earlier. Evelyn's parents came to this country 2 years before, and at that time Evelyn and her sister stayed behind with their grandmother. The reasons for referral to the school social work intern were that, according to teachers, Evelyn had difficulties making new friends, had poor school performance, and displayed low self-esteem. When she met with the intern, they conversed in Spanish, since the intern was also an immigrant from Latin America. During the interview, Evelyn was frequently tearful and reported that it was hard for her to make new friends; she thought she had nothing interesting to say to her classmates. As a result, she spent most of her time alone.

Although cognitive restructuring might have been helpful for Evelyn to examine the validity of the belief that she had nothing interesting to say, the social work intern decided to focus on helping Evelyn with her social skills. They started in the first session with some basic skills—making eye contact with other classmates, smiling at least once when in conversation, complimenting the other person ("I like your shirt"), and revealing some personal information ("I'm having a hard time with chemistry, too"). Evelyn named some specific instances in which she could practice these new skills (at the lunch table, while waiting for classes to start, while waiting for the bus to pick her up in the afternoon). They then rehearsed a couple of possible examples.

The school social worker met with Evelyn the following week, and Evelyn reported that she had been able to practice at least one social skill per day as they had agreed. She realized that when she made friendly overtures, other people typically responded in kind.

They went on to the topic of how to make conversation. Since Evelyn enjoyed watching TV and listening to music, she noted that these could be topics of conversations with others ("Did you see *Charmed* last night?" "What's your favorite show?" "Who do you like to listen to?"). She also could talk about a situation that she had in common with another person. For example, since her bus was often late in the afternoon, she could talk to the other students at the bus stop about this. Again, the intern rehearsed the skills with Evelyn, who indicated specific people with whom she was interested in starting a conversation. Evelyn enjoyed the role plays and was smiling when she left the next session.

The next time they met, Evelyn said that she'd been nervous but had followed through with the assignment of initiating at least one new conversation per day. She also reported that she now has lunch with classmates and that she felt particularly attracted to three other students who seemed to be returning an interest in friendship. At this point, although the social work continued to monitor Evelyn's socializing, they moved to another goal, to help Evelyn with her school performance.

Exercise 7-15

Do you have a client who needs help with social skills? Assess the skills that are needed and do training with the client on these skills. Rate the person's comfort level on a scale of 1 to 10 on each particular skill before and after your training.

Putting It All Together: Developing a Coping Plan

We have so far discussed skills singularly, but with complex problems, many skills are called upon. In Chapter 1, we discussed that there are often many antecedents to behaviors, and we spent considerable time delineating triggers of a particular problematic behavior. In a coping plan, the triggers for a particular behavior are examined, and ways to avoid, change, or cope with those triggers are discussed.

EXAMPLE 7-5

Jennifer, whose family is currently under child protective services monitoring, neglected her children due to her addiction to alcohol and crack cocaine. The social worker examined her triggers for substance abuse in the different domains (social, environmental, physical, emotional, cognitive) and helped Jennifer develop a plan based on those triggers.

Social Cue

Jennifer has many friends with whom she uses drugs.

Coping Plan

Avoidance. Jennifer can be taught how to avoid friends with whom she "parties" (e.g., not calling or visting them, not returning their phone calls, and staying inside when they might be out on the streets).

Self-Talk. "My children come first. I can do this. I am making the right choice."

Communication Skills. Jennifer can learn how to resist the offers of friends to use alcohol and drugs.

Social Skills. Jennifer can learn how to use skills to meet people who don't use substances.

Environmental Cue

Jennifer lives in an impoverished urban neighborhood where drugs are easily accessible.

Coping Plan

Avoidance. As above, Jennifer can avoid certain places where drugs are being sold.

Self-Talk. For situations that are unavoidable, Jennifer can use self-talk: "I'm just going to walk by that house. I can do this. My children come first. I want to stay out of trouble. I want to show my kids the right way to live."

Problem-Solving Skills. Jennifer can use the problem-solving process to determine her options for raising income or tapping into other resources so she can live in a different neighborhood.

Emotional Cue

When Jennifer is depressed, she uses alcohol and/or drugs to give herself a lift.

Coping Plan

Self-Talk. "These feelings don't last long—they never do. This will pass soon."

Cognitive Restructuring. Jennifer can learn how to target the negative beliefs that underlie her depression and substitute more positive and realistic thoughts.

Communication Skills. Communication skills can help Jennifer talk to people about her feelings and to make behavior change requests when their actions are bringing her down.

Problem-Solving Skills. Jennifer can problem-solve on different strategies to manage her depressed moods.

Cognitive Cue

Jennifer has thoughts such as, "I don't know how I'm going to manage without getting high. I've got too much stress going on. I need drugs."

Coping Plan

Cognitive Restructuring. This involves recognizing these automatic thoughts, challenging them, and replacing them with more positive thoughts, such as "Getting high has led to more problems than anything else. Plenty of people manage in life without getting high. I'm learning how to do this. It just feels unfamiliar right now."

Exercise 7-16

Take your assessment on triggers in Chapter 1 (exercise 1–4) and develop a plan for coping, using the Coping Plan for Cues worksheet.

WORKSHEET 7–3 **Coping Plan for Cues**

Domain	Cues	Intervention
Social		
Environmental		
Emotional		
Cognitive		
Physical		

Summary

This chapter focused on behaviorally based skills that can help people manage the stressors and challenges that come up in their daily lives. At the conclusion of the chapter, you saw how the coping skills can be put together to manage the type of complex problems with which people grapple. By reading the material, working through the exercises, and applying the skills with clients, your own skill level has hopefully also developed.

References

Beach, S., Sandeen, E., & O'Leary, K. (1990). *Depression in marriage: A model for etiology and treatment*. New York: Guilford.

Clarke, G., Lewinsohn, P., & Hops, H. (1990). The adolescent coping with depression course. Online: http://www.kpchr.org/public/acwd/acwd.html. Accessed August 2, 2004.

Compas, B., Connor-Smith, J., Saltzman, H., Thomsen, A. H., & Wadsworth, M. (2001). Coping with stress during childhood and adolescence: Problems, progress, and potential in theory and research. *Psychological Bulletin, 127*, 87–127.

Cordova, J., and Jacobson, N. (1993). Couple distress. In D. H. Barlow (Ed.), *Clinical handbook of psychological disorders: A step-by-step treatment manual*, 2nd ed. (pp. 481–512). New York: Guilford.

Davis, M., Eshelman, E. R., & McKay, M. (1995). *The relaxation and stress reduction workbook*. New York: MFJ Books.

Deblinger, E., & Heflin, A. H. (1996). *Treating sexually abused children and their nonoffending parents: A cognitive-behavioral approach*. Thousand Oaks, CA: Sage.

D'Zurilla, T., & Nezu, A. (2001). Problem-solving therapies. In K. Dobson & S. Keith (Eds.), *Handbook of cognitive-behavioral therapies*, 2nd ed. (pp. 211–245). New York: Guilford.

Foster, S., & Robin, A. (1998). Parent-adolescent conflict and relationship discord. In E. Mash & R. Barkley (Eds.), *Treatment of childhood disorders*, 2nd ed. (pp. 601–646). New York: Guilford.

Wheeler, J., Christensen, A., & Jacobson, N. (2001). Couple distress. In D. Barlow (Ed.), *Clinical handbook of psychological disorders: A step-by-step treatment manual*, 3rd ed. New York: Guilford.

8

— ▼▲▼ —

Conveying Information in a Collaborative Way

This chapter describes a collaborative approach to skill-building. That is, rather than educating clients about skills in a lecturing format, the social worker delivers information in a way that is attentive to a client's levels of engagement, comprehension, and capabilities so that intervention will be made useful and relevant for that particular person (Carroll, 1998). The foundation for the skills training that will take place is the relationship the social worker builds with the client. The social worker must facilitate a supportive alliance so that the client feels safe to learn new behaviors.

The guidelines for collaborative skill-building are illustrated in this chapter with child behavior management techniques. However, these same guidelines can be applied to other problems. See, for example, Carroll (1998), who has written about treating cocaine use disorders.

1. *What has the person already tried?* Before giving out information, the social worker needs to know how the person has already tried to handle his or her difficulties. Asking about problem-solving attempts gives people credit for their efforts and a sense of their own competence. The social worker also acquires important information for intervention purposes. First, the social worker learns about what has been tried and in what ways: "When you say you used time-out, tell me, what did you do? What happened?" The social

worker may find that efforts were applied inconsistently or in a manner that sabotaged the client's success. Sometimes people may have to be educated about a more effective way to apply possible solutions. Second, if strategies have been applied correctly but have still not been helpful, the social worker may suggest avoiding the same tactics and trying a different approach (Murphy, 1997). This process of asking questions about clients' previous problem-solving attempts contributes toward building a collaborative alliance about the best course of action that will take place.

EXAMPLE 8-1

We first learned about Sonya in Chapter 1, Example 1-1. Sonya was HIV-infected and the mother of three children. She was having problems managing 8-year-old Ellie's behavior. To the intern's question about what approaches Sonya has tried to get Ellie to obey her, Sonya said she's "tried everything." When the intern pressed for more detail, Sonya said that she had tried time-out, but that Ellie just sat on the stairway. "It's impossible to get her to do anything I say." The intern explored further the use of Sonya's time-out and found out that Sonya was trying to send Ellie to her room, a place she shared with her sister and where there were plenty of toys and activities. She also discovered that Sonya, after screaming at her daughter to get into "time-out," would give up on getting her to go there.

   The intern went on to ask about Sonya's other problem-solving attempts. Sonya said, "I'll take away privileges, like they're not allowed to watch TV." But she said that wasn't helpful either because "the house is so small, they just end up watching the TV anyway." After this conversation, the intern complimented Sonya for her efforts in trying to get the children's behavior under control. Sonya responded favorably to the praise. The intern had also learned some important information. She could see that Sonya might need more training on these techniques, with problem solving focused on some of the barriers to implementation. She also noted that Sonya primarily relied upon punishment and wasn't making effective use of praise and other reinforcement.

Finally, the social work intern was well acquainted with this case and knew the family had been under considerable stress. Not only was there Sonya's HIV infection, but she had also been hospitalized a year ago for an aneurysm. During her hospital stay, the children's stepfather had let the children stay with a family friend, and according to Sonya, this person let the children do whatever they wanted. Since her return from the hospital, Sonya felt that she had lost control of her kids, particularly Ellie, because for 6 months they had lived with no boundaries or rules. The intern noted that the family might find communication skills helpful so they could discuss with each other the stressors that had occurred in the past and the ones they were still living with.

2. *Avoid using technical explanations.* The words *learning* or *rewards*, for instance, can be used instead of *reinforcement, contingencies,* and *stimulus conditions* to make information more understandable.

3. *Pay attention to clients' verbal and nonverbal cues.* These might include lack of eye contact, one-word responses, or yawning. ("I notice that you keep yawning, and I was wondering what your thoughts are on what we're talking about today.")

4. *Ask people to describe the skill in their own words.* ("We've talked a lot about having the kids take a time-out when they're misbehaving. Just to make sure you're confident about what you can do, can you tell me what you plan to do when they are fighting with each other and won't stop?")

5. *Elicit clients' reactions to the material.* ("What do you think about these ideas?")

6. *Elicit clients' views on how they might use particular skills.* ("Now that we've talked about reinforcement, what do you think would work best for you?")

7. *Ask clients to provide concrete examples of situations in which strategies or skills can be applied.* ("Can you think of a time last week when your children did that?")

8. *Offer a cluster of options so the client can choose a course of action from among alternatives.* ("Let me describe a few possibilities, and you tell me which of these makes the most sense for you.")

9. *Employ frequent modeling and behavioral rehearsal.* The procedures for role plays are detailed extensively in Chapter 2.

10. *Give feedback in normative terms.* ("I have another parent I'm working with. She was waiting all week to give her children their reward, but then she realized that a week was too long, and they were too young to remember what they were working toward." [Azar & Ferraro, 2000].)

11. *Use appropriate self-disclosure.* A collaborative approach further makes use of self-disclosure when appropriate. For example, if a social worker is teaching behavior management skills, bringing up some of her own parenting challenges and solutions may help parents feel that the social worker understands their present circumstances.

12. *Use humor when appropriate.*

13. *Employ physical and concrete prompts.* For example, suggest that clients write down task, and goals, or that they place signs in high-traffic areas in the home as reminders of new skills.

14. *Use adult analogies to help parents understand information.* ("If you worked all day making a nice dinner for your boyfriend and afterwards he didn't say anything, would you do it again?" [Azar & Ferraro, 2000, p. 438].) Selekman (1999) uses an exercise with parents in which they are asked to list the characteristics of their best and worst supervisor. From this exercise, parents often see the importance of praise and reward and the problems with criticism, yelling, and physical punishment.

15. *Validate frustration with new material.* ("This is a lot to take in, but you're doing great.")

16. **Work with the client in brief time periods more frequently.** As opposed to a social worker in a therapist role, a social worker in a hospital, child welfare, or other crisis-oriented setting sometimes has briefer chunks of time to spend with clients and can be more flexible about the number of contacts.

17. **Reframe the time and effort investment in learning new skills.** ("Although it does take work to learn something new, it pays off down the road when you know what to do to keep your children in line. Then you won't have to work as hard and get as stressed out.")

18. **Compliment people extensively.** ("You did a good job." "I liked the way you said that.")

19. **Offer rewards to parents for following through with skills.** Such rewards night include meals at fast-food restaurants, toys for the children, or a positive report at the next court date.

20. **Use deductive questioning.** Deductive questioning is designed to help clients figure out connections between their behaviors and their children's learning. For instance, when parents "give in" after setting a consequence, ask, "I wonder what your child learned in that situation."

EXAMPLE 8-2

In Chapter 3, Example 3-1, the social worker at a long-term care facility trained a nurse and her staff on how to manage the noncompliant behavior of one of their patients, Michael. The social worker used several ways to teach skills collaboratively. These are demonstrated here:

Using Adult Analogies

The nurse, Alison, was frustrated that her patient, Michael, hadn't met more of his goals in the first week: "I expected him to do more. I also started thinking that I shouldn't have to encourage him so strongly as if he's doing me a favor! I'm only doing what's best for him. Maybe I should just leave this social work stuff to you."

The social worker gently pointed out that most people depend on rewards and reinforcement in the course of their daily lives. For example, when Alison provided Michael with positive reinforcement, it was the equivalent of the director of nursing telling Alison that she had done a good job or that her work was appreciated.

The social worker used another analogy to address Alison's disappointment that Michael had not reached all of his goals. She knew Alison was the mother of three children and asked her if she was always successful in getting them to do something on their own, especially when it was something they weren't in the habit of doing. Alison realized immediately where the social worker was going and responded, "I guess I was expecting too much the first time around. After all, I've been trying to get Michael out of bed and in the shower for quite a while. I guess I should be glad he got out of bed the one time he did. When I look at it that way, the positive reinforcement did work."

Offering Frequent Compliments

Continuing from the above situation, the social worker congratulated Alison on her ability to find the positive in what she previously viewed to be a negative situation. She also validated Alison's own long-term nursing skills, as well as her know-how as a mother, stating that Alison's experiences were a valuable contribution. The social worker further complimented Alison on her use of positive reinforcement with Michael and on her ability to educate other staff members, as the social worker had overheard the nurse aides on several occasions reinforcing Michael's efforts.

Maintaining Optimism About the Change Process

Social worker: Alison, you really did well. You successfully ignored Michael when he was noncompliant and then praised him when he was.

Alison: Well, I didn't do it all the time. In fact, one time I got quite angry with him and said "Michael!" in a furious voice and stormed out.

Social worker: What were your thoughts following that incident?

Alison: That I had blown it after being so careful!

Social worker: But you immediately recognized what you had done. You solved part of the problem just by being aware of your responses. And then you were success- ful in your efforts to use praise and extinction through- out the rest of that day. I'm proud of you.

Using Humor

Recall that in a moment of frustration, Alison had said, "Maybe I should just leave this social work stuff to you." After the social worker had used some of the other collaborative techniques, she joked to Alison, "You see, you are good with this social work stuff."

Validating the Person's Experience

When the social worker had first asked about the week's progress, Alison sharply reminded the social worker that Michael was not her only patient and that she was extremely busy. Rather than becom- ing defensive, the social worker conveyed her understanding of Alison's heavy patient load and the effort she was making.

Reframe the Time and Energy Investment for Learning New Strategies

To Alison's statement that she was busy, the social worker offered the following reframe: "Maybe you can look at it this way—the time you take to learn these techniques may actually save you time and energy in the long run. For instance, you and your staff now don't have to spend time and energy arguing with patients. I'm sure Michael is not your only patient who acts like this. And when you do have a person like this on your floor, it causes staff a good deal of aggravation. Also, the health consequences to noncompliance with the medical regime may lead to bigger issues for you to deal with down the line."

These examples show how the social worker taught techniques in a way that took into account the realities of the nurse's situation. She was encouraging and optimistic about change in the face of these realities, however, adopting her approach as needed to the circumstances and the nurse's level of engagement.

Exercise 8-1

A social work intern provided in-home services to Liza, a Caucasian woman with mild mental retardation. Liza was having problems managing her 4-year-old son Will's behavior. A social work intern started by teaching Liza how to make effective commands. The intern went through the process of explaining them to Liza, but she said it was difficult because of Liza's cognitive level. She said that Liza didn't appreciate the necessity of verbal communication. Instead, Will was used to pointing for what he wanted and hitting, punching, and crying to get his point across. The intern also complained that since she only saw Liza and Will in the home once a week, it was not enough for Liza to learn this new skill. If you were working with Liza, what methods would you use to help her learn effective command-giving?

Exercise 8-2

Take three of the guidelines for teaching skills in a collaborative way and apply them to your work with a client. What impact did implementing these guidelines have? If you do not have a client to whom you are teaching skills, consider a client from a past caseload, a hypothetical client, or a classmate's client, and follow the same process.

How to Work with Entrenched Beliefs

In this section, we examine cases in which the client has difficulty learning a new behavior because of firmly held beliefs about the "right" way to do something that may not be in his or her best interests. Also pertinent to this topic are Chapter 4, which examines how to work with people's belief systems, and Chapter 9, on how to help people build their motivation to change. We use the example of physical punishment, continuing with the focus of this chapter on parent management techniques.

Punishment

People's beliefs about the necessity for physical punishment often get in the way of their learning new skills. The following questions, devised by Webster-Stratton and Herbert (1993), explore such beliefs in a sensitive fashion. As the client responds, the social worker can then provide education about the disadvantages of physical punishment without resorting to lectures.

1. *Tell me how spanking works for you. What do you see as its advantages?* People tend to feel less resistant when they are allowed to talk about what they get out of the problem behavior. The discussion also helps the social worker understand the functions the behavior serves so that he or she can deliver more effective interventions.

Parents often say that they use punishment because it teaches their children a lesson or that it makes them behave. However, what they don't realize is that they are teaching their children to escalate their misbehavior until physical punishment is implemented. Parents are also being negatively reinforced for physical punishment (Kazdin, 2001). In behavioral terms, the principle involved is *negative reinforcement*; the removal of a coercive event (child misbehavior) through parent behavior (physical punishment) reinforces the behavior (physical abuse) responsible for removing the coercive event (Kazdin, 2001).

Parents sometimes report that they use physical punishment because they want their children to know "who's in charge" and to show them respect. The social worker can affirm the intent of the behavior rather than the behavior itself and emphasize the importance of authoritative parenting, which involves having and enforcing clear and consistent rules, as well as monitoring children's whereabouts and activities (Steinberg, 2001). Authoritative parenting can also be affirmed when people say they employ hitting because they want children to succeed in life and to be tough against adversity. Parents should be advised that the effects of physical punishment fail to carry over to situations where it is not applied; for instance, the child might eventually comply at home, but not at school, where corporal punishment is not typically used. Therefore, children are not learning from physical punishment in ways that teach them how to behave in settings, such as school, that are important for their success.

At times, parents rationalize physical punishment in terms of the way their parents disciplined them. At this point, you can explore society's changing mores toward physical punishment. This depersonalizes the discussion, explaining it in terms of societal attitudes instead.

Another tactic to take when parents talk about having been physically punished by their parents, yet they "turned out all right," is to ask about the subsequent result on the relationship between them and their parents. You might also ask about what they want to have different for their children than they experienced themselves.

2. *How often do you use it?* Parents often say that they use physical punishment "only when they have to." Unfortunately, this pattern actually trains children to escalate their disobedience until physical punishment is threatened or actually used. In addition, the intensity of punishment does not translate into increased results (Kazdin, 2001).

3. *How do you feel afterwards?* Some parents report feeling remorse for hurting their children. The social worker can channel such feelings into motivation to learn new techniques. Kazdin (2001) reports that while the original purpose of punishment is to reduce noncompliance and teach appropriate behavior, in actuality, negative reinforcement, the satisfaction parents get from "teaching the child a lesson," the reduction of parental frustration, and the exacting of "revenge" on the child play larger roles. For parents who get a sense of satisfaction from releasing anger at the child, the social worker can assist them in developing awareness of when anger builds and on how to de-escalate triggers and tension, so that their child does not become a target for their rage.

4. *How does your child feel about physical punishment?* After the client has responded to this question, the social worker can provide some education about the impact of physical punishment on children (Kazdin, 2001):

- Children may feel negatively toward the person enacting the punishment and the behaviors for which they are being punished. Children often feel resentful of siblings, for instance, when they have been physically punished for fighting with them.
- Children may avoid the consequences of punishment by lying about behaviors.

- It teaches children aggression by modeling aggression.
- Punishment may teach children what they shouldn't do, but not what they should do.
- Research findings indicate physical abuse is correlated for children with (1) aggression/behavior problems; (2) poor impulse control; (3) social skills deficits; (4) cognitive deficits in terms of language and IQ/academic problems; (5) trauma-related symptoms, such as anxiety and depression (Kolko & Swensen, 2002). Adolescents physically abused as children exhibit more externalizing behaviors and violent criminal offending compared to their non–physically abused counter-parts (Malinosky-Rummell & Hansen, 1993). Longer-term conse-quences for adults include the following: among men, increased rates of violence, including criminal offenses; among women, internalizing problems, such as self-abuse, suicidality, dissociation, somatization, depression, and anxiety.

5. *Do you ever feel you lose control when you spank?* Most parents do suffer a loss of control during physical punishment because the purpose, as we dis-cussed, often most involves the satisfaction parents get from "teaching the child a lesson," the reduction of parental frustration, and the exacting of revenge on the child.

6. *Are there any disadvantages?* This question allows any other doubts about physical punishment to arise if they haven't already done so. A chief disadvan-tage for many parents will be their involvement in child protective services systems for the use of physical punishment.

Exercise 8-3

Do you work with clients who hold certain beliefs that are against mainstream norms and values and/or are against their best interest? Use the above process to get a particular client to explore these beliefs. (If your case is not specific to physical punishment, you can use the point-counterpoint technique discussed in Chapter 4.) If you do not have a client who is appropriate for this exercise, conduct a role play with a fellow student who has such a client. Write out in summary fashion the "client's" responses. How did the client's beliefs shift as a result of this process?

Homework

A critical aspect of cognitive-behavioral interventions is that people practice the strategies they are taught. Because cognitive-behavioral therapy is a skills-oriented approach, people learn skills not just by talking with a social worker, but by putting them into action. As with any learning, it is expected that there will be mistakes along the way and that attainment of new information will be gradual.

Carroll (1998) recommends that a practitioner provide a rationale for homework, such as the following:

> It will be important for us to talk about and work on new coping skills in our sessions, but it is even more important to put these skills into use in your daily life. You are really the expert on what works and doesn't work for you, and the best way to find out what works for you is to try it out. It's very important that you give yourself a chance to try out new skills outside our sessions so we can identify and discuss any problems you might have putting them into practice. We've found, too, that people who try to practice these things tend to do better in treatment. The practice exercises I'll be giving you at the end of each session will help you try out these skills. We'll go over how well they worked for you, what you thought of the exercises, and what you learned about yourself and your coping style at the beginning of each session.

Rather than assuming that clients will complete a particular exercise for homework, the social worker should assess commitment to a task that the client and the social worker have collaboratively devised. Again, we return to a 1-to-10 scale to evaluate how much the client is likely to follow through. Anything less than a 7 indicates that further exploration might be needed (Hepworth, Rooney, & Larsen, 2002). A client might not see the value of the task, or he or she might not understand it. The client also might be ambivalent about the goal of the intervention or participating in intervention, which may warrant the social worker switching strategies (see working collaboratively in this chapter, Chapter 9 on building motivation, or Chapter 1 on setting goals).

It is critical when developing tasks to gain client input, to offer choices and practice, and to anticipate any obstacles that might come up (Carroll,

1998). Problem-solving techniques may be necessary (see Chapter 7). Overcoming barriers may involve a novel way to approach the task (e.g., using a tape recorder to record dysfunctional thoughts and their replacements instead of writing). Asking another person for assistance can also be suggested. Several examples of this type of work follow.

Recall the example of Emma, who had her hand amputated (see Chapter 5, Example 5–7). In this case, the social work intern at the hospital suggested that she use a tape recorder to record her negative thoughts and her thought replacements. Another example involves Paula (Example 5–6). Although Paula was agreeable to homework tasks—the progression of Lou Gehrig disease had taken so much out of her control that having an assignment to complete helped her feel more in control—but she could no longer write. The social worker therefore offered to stop by Paula's room at the end of each day; Paula could then recount her thoughts, and the social worker would write them down.

In Chapter 2, Example 2–3, the case of Daryl was described. He was paralyzed on one side of his body due to a shooting that had occurred 4 years before. Daryl was to receive bus tickets for following through with his community referrals. Daryl's responsibility was to attend the appointments; yet the social work intern had to figure out a way to track these meetings, especially since she was only at the agency twice a week. To handle this problem, she called upon a coworker to distribute the bus tickets on the other three days of the week. In order to verify his appointments, the intern initially tried calling the person with whom he was meeting. However, she found it difficult to reach the particular person involved. The client and the intern then decided that he would bring a copy of her business card with him and ask the person meeting with him to leave a message on her machine that he had indeed kept his appointment. The other barrier the intern encountered was that sometimes Daryl would ask other staff members for bus tickets, and they would give them to him. Therefore, the intern had to make a weekly reminder in staff meetings to the other caseworkers about the system he was on.

Another important aspect of homework is that the social worker follows up during the next contact about it. Carroll (1998) suggests that at least 5 minutes should be spent discussing the assignment, preferably at the beginning of the contact. If the social worker does not attend to tasks, clients will conclude that they are not important and will not take them seriously.

When people say that they were unable to complete or did not get to the agreed-upon task, the social worker should reinforce homework behavior rather than noncompliance. By saying "Oh, that's okay," or "No problem," the social worker gives clients the message that tasks are not important. Instead, time should be spent reviewing obstacles that came up and negotiating the task for the following week. It could be, for instance, that the task was too ambitious for the client, and it needs to be broken down into smaller, more manageable pieces. Other possible reasons for noncompliance include clients' sense of hopelessness about change and their presumption that willpower alone will work (Carroll, 1998). Clients' lives often are chaotic and crisis-ridden, and some clients are not sufficiently organized to complete tasks. By identifying the specific problem, the social worker can help the client work through it.

Webster-Stratton and Herbert (1993) offer a series of recommended questions to ask when the client has difficulty following through with tasks.

- What makes it hard for you to do the assignment?
- How have you overcome this problem in the past?
- What advice would you give to someone else who has this problem?
- What can you do to make it easier for you to complete the assignment this week?
- What assignment might be more useful for you?
- What thoughts come to mind when you think about this assignment?
- Does this assignment seem relevant to your life?
- How could we make this assignment more helpful to you?

If the task did not work out as planned, the social worker should convey that there is no such thing as a failure. Instead, the focus can be on, "What did you learn? What needs to be done differently next time?" This approach encourages the client to continue testing out new skills and activities.

This chapter provides many ways to address clients' follow-through with skills learned in sessions. If these strategies are not successful, the social worker may need to go through the problem-solving process with the client (see Chapter 7) in order to find solutions for how the person can complete between-session tasks.

Exercise 8-4

Considering the information on having clients complete between-contact tasks, discuss a case in which a client had difficulty following through with an agreed-upon task. Which strategies did you use? What innovations did you come up with for handling barriers? What was the impact of your work on the client's completion of homework?

Handling Lack of Cooperation

This chapter and Chapter 9, "Building Motivation," discuss how to engage the client so that cooperation is enhanced. This chapter concludes with some other strategies for handling clients' "uncooperative behaviors" (particularly adolescents and other nonvoluntary clients), including (but certainly not limited to) lack of response and blaming others. Certain tools enable the social worker to respond to such stances in a calm manner so that responsibility for change is placed on the client and work proceeds in a productive way.

First consider the following options for dealing with the "I don't know" response that some clients take when faced with questions:

1. Allow silence (about 20 to 30 seconds).
2. Rephrase the question.
3. Ask a relationship question ("What does your mother say about your leaving the house at night?") (de Jong & Berg, 2001). Sometimes people feel put on the spot by having to answer questions about themselves but can take the perspective of others and view their behavior from this perspective.
4. Say, "I know you don't know, so just make it up," which bypasses the resistance or the fear that clients don't know or don't have the right answer. Or, using presuppositional language, say "Suppose you did know. . . ."
5. Speak hypothetically about others: "What would (prosocial peers that the person respects) say they do to keep out of trouble (or get passing grades or get along with their parents)?"

There are also options for responding when clients blame others and fail to take responsibility for their actions.

1. Bertolino and O'Hanlon (2002) suggest that practitioners reflect the client's statements back, leaving out the part they perceive as making them unaccountable for their actions, as was done with Cheryl when discussing her anger management issues at school and at home.

   Cheryl: He called me a name, so I hit him.
   Social worker: You hit him.
   Cheryl: My foster mother yelled at me, so I yelled back.
   Social worker: You yelled at your foster mother.

2. Explore the details of the context (Bertolino & O'Hanlon, 2002; de Jong & Berg, 2001): "What are you doing when your foster mother is talking to you in a normal tone?" "What are you doing when your teacher treats you with respect?" "What are you doing when the girls in your neighborhood are leaving you alone?" This technique allows clients to

see that they are part of a reciprocal interaction process in which their behaviors influence those of others, and vice versa.

Summary

The tools presented in this chapter can help the social worker engage more effectively and can also be used throughout the change process when "unco-operative" or "resistant" behaviors occur. The stance taken in this book follows from the principles of motivational interviewing (see Chapter 9)—that rather than being the problem of the client, "resistance" is a signal to the social worker that he or she needs to adjust change strategies.

Since a certain level of cooperation is required for the successful imple-mentation of cognitive-behavioral interventions, the social worker has to attend, through collaborative strategies, to building and maintaining the client's engagement in the process, taking into account the client's level of motivation, comprehension, and capabilities. This chapter also described a process for sensitively exploring client convictions and beliefs about the "right" way to do things, so that people can perhaps become more open to learning new skills. Finally, this chapter focused on how to encourage task completion, because learning skills is heavily dependent on practice outside the session and generalization to real-world settings.

References

Azar, S., & Ferraro, M. (2000). How can parenting be enhanced? In H. Dubowitz & D. DePanfilis (Eds.), *Handbook for child protection practice* (pp. 437–624). Thousand Oaks, CA: Sage.

Bertolino, B., & O'Hanlon, B. (2002). *Collaborative, competency-based counseling and therapy*. Boston, MA: Allyn & Bacon.

Carroll, K. (1998). *A cognitive-behavioral approach: Treating cocaine addiction*. Online: http://www.drugabuse.gov/TXManuals/CBT/CBT1.html. Accessed August 28, 2004.

De Jong, P., & Berg, I. K. (2001). *Interviewing for solutions*, 2nd ed. Pacific Grove, CA: Brooks/Cole.

Hepworth, D. H., Rooney, R., & Larsen, J. (2002). *Direct social work practice: Theory and skills*, 6th ed. Belmont, CA: Brooks/Cole.

Kazdin, A. (2001). *Behavior modification in applied settings*, 6th ed. Pacific Grove, CA: Brooks/Cole.

Kolko, D. J., & Swenson, C. C. (2002). *Assessing and treating physically abused children and their families: A cognitive-behavioral approach.* Thousand Oaks, CA: Sage.

Malinosky-Rummell, R., & Hansen, D. J. (1993). Long-term consequences of childhood physical abuse. *Psychological Bulletin, 114*, 68–79.

Murphy, J. (1997). *Solution-focused counseling in middle and high schools.* Alexandria, VA: American Counseling Association.

Selekman, M. (1999). The solution-oriented parenting group revisited. *Journal of Systemic Therapies, 18*(1): 5–23.

Steinberg, L. 2001. We know some things: Parent-adolescent relationships in retrospect and prospect. *Journal of Research on Adolescence 11*, 1–19.

Webster-Stratton, C., & Herbert, M. (1993). What really happens in parent training? *Behavior Modification, 17*, 407–457.

9

—▼▲▼—

Building Motivation

This chapter discusses the use of motivational interviewing for clients who are not yet ready to take action with cognitive-behavioral interventions. Motivational interviewing is a brief treatment model (one to four sessions) formulated to produce rapid change in which the client's motivation is mobilized. Motivational interviewing avoids prescriptive techniques and training the client in skills; instead the client's own motivation is galvanized (Miller & Rollnick, 2002). Motivational interviewing is suggested when clients are initially low in motivation for change. The backdrop for motivational interviewing is the transtheoretical stages of change model. The stages of change model conceptualizes that people need different interventions, depending on their level of motivation to change. Because the stages of change model is important for understanding the context for motivational interviewing, this model is first described. Note that in only certain stages are cognitive-behavioral techniques recommended.

Stages of Change Model

In acknowledgment of the reluctance of many substance abusers to change their patterns, Prochaska and colleagues (Connors, Donovan, & DiClemente, 2001; Prochaska & Norcross, 1994) developed the transtheoretical stages of change model. The model allows for many different theoretical approaches, but employed at the point where they will be most effective. Six stages of change have been formulated:

1. Precontemplation
2. Contemplation
3. Determination
4. Action
5. Maintenance
6. Relapse

Particular techniques from different theoretical orientations match the relevant stage of change with a primary focus on building motivation to get individuals to take action toward their goals and to maintain changes.

Precontemplation

In precontemplation, the individual believes there is no problem behavior and therefore is unwilling to do anything about it. At this stage, the individual sees the problem behavior as possessing more advantages than disadvantages. Typically, individuals in this stage are defensive and resistant about their behavior. They lack awareness of the problem, and if in treatment, are usually coerced or pressured to do so by others. In treatment, they are unwilling to participate (Connors, Donovan, & DiClemente, 2001).

When a client is in precontemplation, the social worker should probably avoid approaches such as cognitive-behavioral therapy that focus on behavioral change. Instead, the practitioner should work on building the client's motivation to change and on increasing awareness of the negative aspects of the problem behavior. Motivational interviewing techniques are an ideal intervention at this stage. In order to move to the next stage, the advantages of changing should outweigh the disadvantages of changing.

The social worker can also expose the client in precontemplation to forces of social liberation, which offers people information about the problem and public support for change efforts. Much of this involves harnessing the forces that are already present to help people with problem behaviors. For example, a large self-help network exists for problems ranging from substance use, overeating, and mental disorders.

Contemplation

In contemplation, individuals begin to recognize that there is a problem and to consider the feasibility and costs of changing the behavior. They want to understand their behavior and frequently feel distress over it. During this stage, individuals think about making change in the next 6 months. While they may have made attempts to change their behavior in the past, they are not yet prepared to take action at this point; they are engaged in the process of evaluating the advantages and disadvantages of the problem (Connors, Donovan, & DiClemente, 2001).

The social worker's role during this stage is to continue to bolster the client's motivation. The social worker can also educate the client on the problem behavior and the recovery process. Some cognitive-behavioral techniques might be helpful during this stage. Self-monitoring of problem behavior may be employed so that the individual can gain awareness of the frequency and intensity of the behavior, the cues that elicit problem behavior, and the consequences that follow. Identifying social support systems are critical during this change so that others can promote change efforts.

Determination

In determination (also called preparation), the individual is poised to change in the next month. Cognitive-behavioral techniques may be used in earnest during this stage. Readiness to change should be bolstered. Goals can be set with a change plan developed (Connors, Donovan, & DiClemente, 2001). In order to be prepared to resist problem behaviors, the individual should develop and rehearse coping skills, such as relaxation training, visualization of successful outcomes, cognitive restructuring, communication skills, and avoidance of environmental cues, before being placed in high-risk situations.

Action

In action, the individual has started to modify the problem behavior and/or the environment in an effort to promote change in the past 6 months. The individual at this point is willing to follow suggested strategies and activities for change (Connors, Donovan, & DiClemente, 2001). In the action stage, the social worker should strive toward maintaining client engagement and supporting a realistic view of change through helping the individual achieve small, successive steps. The social worker should acknowledge and empathize with the difficulties associated with the early stages of change. Appraisal of high-risk situations and coping strategies to overcome these are a mainstay of this stage. Alternative reinforcers to problem behaviors should also be applied. Assessment of social support systems continues to be essential so that others are a helpful resource for change rather than a hindrance.

Maintenance

In maintenance, sustained change has occurred for at least 6 months. The individual is working to sustain changes achieved to date. The social worker continues to support lifestyle changes. Attention is focused on avoiding slips or relapses (Prochaska & Norcross, 1994) and helping the individual find alternative sources of satisfaction and enjoyment. The social worker should continue to assist the individual in practicing and applying coping strategies. Awareness should be built around cognitive distortions that might be associated with the problem. For example, if an individual with an alcohol problem begins to think, "Life is no fun without drinking," recognizing this as a high-risk thought is essential so that the validity of the thought can be questioned: "What were the consequences of my drinking? Were they always fun? How else can I experience fun and enjoyment in my life without drinking?"

Maintaining environmental control is critical at this stage. For example, an individual trying to overcome a drinking problem should avoid socializing in bars. As much as possible, the individual should not put temptation in the way. However, he or she should also be armed with the necessary skills to face high-risk situations if they do occur. Continued practice with skills is necessary for this reason.

Relapse

Rather than seen as failure (Connors, Donovan, & DiClemente, 2001), relapse is viewed as an opportunity for greater awareness of high-risk situations and the coping strategies that need developing to address these challenges. The notion that change is a spiral-type process rather than linear in nature means that relapse is just a normal part of the process of change. In other words, there is one step backward for two steps forward.

Motivational Interviewing

As a student or social worker, you might be accustomed to seeing clients who are mandated to attend services. These clients typically are not motivated to change or to put the effort into using cognitive-behavioral techniques. For the most part, cognitive-behavioral intervention is designed for those who are motivated to take action toward changing their behavior. As a result, you might need some way to help clients develop the motivation to take action toward change. Motivational interviewing has been developed for this purpose.

Carroll (1998), who uses motivational interviewing as part of her cognitive-behavioral treatment for cocaine use disorders, describes that motivational interviewing focuses on *why* clients may go about changing their problem, whereas cognitive-behavioral intervention focuses on *how* clients might do so. Therefore, motivational interviewing and cognitive-behavioral therapy may be viewed as complementary (Baer, Kivlahan, & Donovan, 1999), with motivational interviewing beginning the process before turning to cognitive-behavioral skill-building.

Developed over the last 20 years (Dunn, Deroo, & Rivara, 2001), motivational interviewing is "a client-centered, directive method for enhancing intrinsic motivation to change by exploring and resolving ambivalence" (Miller & Rollnick, 2002, p. 25). Developed for the treatment of substance abuse, motivational interviewing is now being applied to other areas of change, such as eating disorders (Moyers & Rollnick, 2002). It has been employed both as a stand-alone treatment and as a way to engage people in other intervention approaches (Walitzer, Dermen, & Connors, 1999).

Motivational interviewing is conducted in a climate of empathic expression with support for client self-efficacy. Client ambivalence during this process is seen as critical to change, and "resistance" is not seen as client pathology, but as an indication that the social worker needs to reassess change strategies (Yahne & Miller, 1999). Therefore, client confrontation is avoided because this is seen as escalating resistance rather than reducing it. The main point of motivational interviewing is not to use direct persuasion but to assist the client in talking himself or herself into changing.

Techniques

Several techniques mark motivational interviewing. The first is cognitive disso-
nance, which is employed throughout the process of motivational interviewing.
When a client is divided in his or her beliefs or actions, the social worker works
to "tip the balance" in favor of change. Part of this process involves developing
discrepancy between the goals and values a person holds and a current problem
behavior. (For example, if a person holds the value that honesty is important but
is lying about the use of substances to others, that is pointed out to the client:
"On the one hand, you believe that being honest is important, and on the other,
you realize that you have been lying to people lately about the amount you're
using.") To take another example, the main life's goal of a young woman who
had been diagnosed with bulimia nervosa was to have children: "On the one
hand, you want to have children in a few years, and on the other, your bingeing
and purging means that you might harm your body and prevent yourself from
reaching this goal, not to mention what these behaviors might do to a growing
fetus."

Exercise 9-1

Consider a client either from your current caseload or the past. Compose a statement that develops discrepancy between his or her stated goals and/or values and a problem behavior.

Another technique in motivational interviewing is to ask *evocative questions*, those that evoke arguments on the client's behalf in favor of change. Evocative questions are posed in four areas: the advantages of the problem behavior, the disadvantages of the problem behavior, the advantages of changing, and the disadvantages of changing. Following is an array of different questions that can be asked under each of these areas. Caveats by Miller and Rollnick (2002) are that questions should be used selectively and that reflective statements make up the bulk of the practitioner's responses (at a three-to-one ratio to questions).

ADVANTAGES OF THE PROBLEM BEHAVIOR

Identify what the person gets out of the problem behavior: What do you get out of this? What do you like about this?

DISADVANTAGES OF THE PROBLEM BEHAVIOR

What does the client see as the disadvantages (or the "not so good things") about the problem? The social worker should elaborate on the disadvantages by asking for specific examples or for descriptions of the last time that a particular disadvantage occurred. Questions to explore the disadvantages of the problem include:

- What worries you about your current situation?
- What makes you think that you need to do something about this problem?
- What difficulties or hassles have you had in relation to this problem?
- What is there about the problem that you or other people might see as reasons for concern?
- In what ways does this concern you?
- How has this stopped you from doing what you want to do in life?
- What do you think will happen if you don't change anything?

When there seems to be little desire for change, another way to elicit change talk is to ask the client to describe the extremes of his or her (or others') concerns. In this sense, querying extremes might help the person imagine the extreme of consequences that might ensue.

- What concerns you the most about this problem in the long run?
- Suppose you continue on as you have been, without changing. What do you imagine are the worst things that might happen to you?
- How much do you know about what can happen if you (continue with the problem behavior) even if you don't see this happening to you?

ADVANTAGES OF CHANGING

Here, the social worker asks questions about what the client sees as the advantages of changing, making sure to selectively reinforce change statements ("You would really like to be in better health again"). The advantages of changing should further be elaborated upon by asking client to detail the difference it would make to have a particular advantage present in his or her life.

- What would be the advantages of making this change?
- How would you like for things to be different?
- What would you like your life to be like 5 years from now?
- If you could make this change immediately, by magic, how might things be better for you?
- The fact that you're here indicates that at least part of you thinks it's time to do something. What are the main reasons you see for making a change?

It also can be useful to imagine the best consequences that could follow from pursuing a change.

- What might be the best results you could imagine if you make a change?
- If you were completely successful in making the changes you want, how would things be different?

DISADVANTAGES OF CHANGING

Clients are finally asked about the disadvantages of changing: "What will you give up by changing? What will you have to do?"

In the decisional balance technique, the answers to these questions are gathered systematically in a chart (see worksheet 9–1). The balance sheet can also be used as a basis for discussion in subsequent sessions and as a springboard for other interventions, some of which are cognitive-behavioral in nature. Cognitive-behavioral strategies may be employed, for instance, to defeat some of the advantages of the problem behavior. If a person states that the advantage of drinking is that it is the only time he has fun, cognitive restructuring may be used to examine the validity of this belief, or problem-solving skills may be taught so that the client finds alternative ways of having fun.

In addition, intermediary goals can be constructed around decreasing the advantages of the problem behavior. For example, if a client says that she drinks and uses drugs to fit in with the people in her community, goals could center around finding another community for her to live, finding alternative interests, and teaching her skills so that she can make new friends and refuse drugs and alcohol.

Exercise 9-2

If you have a client who is feeling ambivalent about changing, go through the decisional balance process with that person. If you do not have a client who might benefit from this process, take a problem you are considering changing in your life or role play with another student who has a client who is ambivalent about change, and go through the decisional balance process. Write the pros and cons of changing versus not changing in the decisional balance worksheet. What did you find the decisional balance accomplished? How can you work with some of the client's perceived advantages from a cognitive-behavioral approach? What techniques would you use and for what purpose?

WORKSHEET **9–1 Decisional Balance**

Benefits of continuing the problem behavior	Costs of continuing the problem behavior	Benefits of changing	Costs of changing

Another class of techniques in motivational interviewing involves those devised to handle client resistance. Strategies such as variations of reflective responses, which have a directive aspect, are used to move potential power struggles toward change instead (Moyers & Rollnick, 2002). Simple reflection is one such strategy. Simple reflection involves acknowledgment of a client's feeling, thought, or opinion so that the client continues to explore his or her problem rather than becoming defensive ("You're not sure you're ready to spend a lot of time changing right now" [Carroll, 1998]). Simple reflection allows further exploration rather than evoking defensiveness.

Amplified reflection goes beyond simple reflection in that the client's statement is acknowledged but in an extreme fashion. The purpose of such a statement is to bring out the side of the client that wants to change. An amplified reflection, such as the statement, "You really like smoking, and you don't think you'll ever want to change," typically has the effect of getting the client to back down from an entrenched position, allowing for the possibility of negotiation about change (Moyers & Rollnick, 2002).

Double-sided reflection reflects both aspects of the client's ambivalence. When people are exploring the possibility of change, they are divided between wanting to change and also wanting to keep the behavior that has become problematic ("You're not sure cocaine is that big a problem, and at the same time, a lot of people who care about you think it is, and getting arrested for drug possession is causing some problems for you" [Carroll, 1998]). Double-sided reflection can also focus the client's attention on the inconsistency between the person's problem behavior and his or her goals and values (Moyers & Rollnick, 2002). For example, "Your relationship is very important to you, and your drug use is causing problems in the relationship." Developing this kind of discrepancy is a key feature of motivational interviewing.

Shifting focus involves moving the client's attention from a potential impasse to avoid becoming polarized from the client's position. When the client begins to argue against what the social worker might feel is the best course, the social worker should immediately shift his or her position and redirect the focus ("I think you're jumping ahead here. We're not talking at this point about your quitting drinking for the rest of your life; let's talk some more about what the best goal is for you and how to go about making it happen"). The general guideline for shifting focus "is to first defuse the initial concern and then direct attention to a more readily workable issue" (Miller & Rollnick, 2002, p. 102).

Agreement with a twist involves agreement with some of the client's message but in a way that then orients the client in the direction toward change ("I can see why you'd be troubled about your arguments with your wife about your use. I wonder what needs to happen so you don't need to keep talking about this").

Reframing involves taking arguments clients use against change and altering the meaning of the information to promote change instead. A common example involves the tendency of drinkers to consume large quantities without experiencing ill effects and loss of control. This tendency is sometimes used as an excuse for why the drinking is not a problem. This excuse is reframed as tolerance of alcohol, which is actually symptomatic of problem drinking (Miller & Rollnick, 2002).

Clarifying free choice involves communicating that it is up to the client whether he or she wants to change rather than getting embroiled in a debate or an argument about what the client must do ("You can decide to take this on now or wait until another time"). "When people perceive that their freedom of choice is being threatened, they tend to react by asserting their liberty. Probably the best antidote for this reaction is to assure the person of what is surely the truth: in the end, it is the client who determines what happens" (Miller & Rollnick, 2002, p. 106).

Paradox involves siding with the client's resistance, which then causes the client to take the other side of the argument for change ("You've convinced me that your problems are insurmountable. There's nothing we can do about them"). Sometimes clients who have been entrenched in a negative position regarding change will start to argue from the other side of their ambivalence for change when the social worker joins with their position.

Exercise 9-3

Consider a recent instance in which a client showed resistance. Write down what he or she said and how you would respond, using one of the strategies described in this section. What might have been the result of your switching tactics?

Once the client starts taking an interest in change, the social worker concentrates on building the client's confidence. The worker should instill optimism about change through posing some of the following questions:

1. What makes you think that if you did decide to make a change, you could do it?
2. What encourages you that you can change if you want to?
3. What do you think would work for you if you decided to change?
4. When else in your life have you made a significant change like this? How did you do it?
5. How confident are you that you can make this change?
6. What personal strengths do you have that will help you succeed?
7. Who could offer you helpful support in making this change?

The worker may have to guide the client past perceived obstacles and fears associated with change to initiate the beginnings of a change plan with some questions as follows:

1. What do you think you might do?
2. What would you be willing to try?
3. Of the options we've mentioned, which one sounds like it fits you best?
4. Never mind the "how" for right now—what do you want to have happen?
5. So what do you intend to do next?
6. How important is this to you? How much do you want to do this?

Note in the last question that the social worker asks the client how important this change is to him or her. Here, it may be helpful to use the *importance ruler*, a 1-to-10 rating of the client's perception of the importance of doing something about the problem. When the client makes a ranking, follow-up questions include

1. "Why are you at a 4 and not zero?"
2. "What would it take for you to go from 4 to 6?"

A confidence ruler can also be constructed, and similar types of questions can be asked around the client's confidence about changing. The aim is to build clients' self-efficacy about their ability to change once they are motivated to do so.

Evidence of Effectiveness

Miller and colleagues performed extensive research studies on motivational interviewing. Dunn, Deroo, and Rivara (2001) quantitatively reviewed 29 studies mainly with substance abuse but also with smoking, HIV-risk reduction, and diet/exercise. Moderate to large effects were found for reducing both substance abuse and substance dependence with maintenance of effects over time. Motivational interviewing was also found to promote engagement in more intensive substance abuse treatment. Although studies have largely been conducted on adults, adolescent substance use also showed significantly positive results from motivational interviewing (Burke, Arkowitz, & Dunn, 2002).

Overall, motivational interviewing was superior to no-treatment control groups and less viable treatments; it was equivalent to more credible alternatives that were often two to three times longer in duration. For example, in the Project Match Research Group study (1997, 1998), 952 individuals with alcohol problems from outpatient clinics and 774 from aftercare treatment were provided with either 12-step facilitation (12 sessions), cognitive-behavioral coping skills therapy (12 sessions), or motivational enhancement therapy (4 sessions). Motivational enhancement fared as well as the other two treatments that were three times as long both at posttest (Project Match Research Group, 1997) and 3 years later (Project Match Research Group, 1998).

As well as for substance use disorders and dual diagnosis of substance use and schizophrenia, motivational interviewing has been effective for health-related behaviors common to diabetes, hypertension, and bulimia nervosa. Only mixed findings, however, have been indicated for the use of motivational interviewing for quitting cigarette use and for increasing physical exercise. Further, no support has been provided for its use in the reduction of HIV-risk behaviors in the studies to date (Burke, Arkowitz, & Dunn, 2002). These reviews indicate that motivational interviewing can be very helpful for many of the types of problems social workers see.

EXAMPLE 9-1

The social work intern in this case had a first-year placement at an HIV clinic. She worked with an African American woman named Shirley, who was HIV-infected. Yvette, Shirley's 15-year-old daughter, had discovered her mother's HIV status by reading a piece of paper from her mother's doctor a year before. She did not confront her mother, but instead went to her grandmother, who pressed Shirley to discuss the matter with Yvette. When Shirley told Yvette she was HIV-positive, Yvette cried, but after that occasion, they never talked about it again. The intern discussed with Shirley her perceptions of the advantages and the disadvantages of talking further with Yvette about her HIV status.

> *Shirley:* She's not the type of person who likes to talk about things. One of these days, I really want to bring it up, to see how she feels. But Yvette's a very private person.

Social work intern: So you really want to know how Yvette
   feels, but it sounds like you have been holding yourself
   back from talking with her about it.

Shirley: Yes, I don't know what it is. I have a hard time being
   honest and talking about things with her. I really don't
   want her worried about me, you know?

Social work intern: Yvette already knows you're HIV-positive.
   What is it you don't want her worried about?

Shirley: I just don't want her to think I'm going to die or
   something. I mean, I'm going to die someday, but I feel
   good now (laughing).

Social work intern: So what I'm hearing is that you're healthy
   now—you feel strong, and you think you'll live a long
   time. I'm also hearing that you're afraid Yvette may
   worry about you, that she may even worry that you're
   going to die soon. What might be some good things
   that would come from your talking to Yvette about
   this?

Shirley was able to think of several positive outcomes that
might come from talking with her daughter about her HIV status,
which included a closer relationship and less potential stress on her
daughter. As for the negatives of continuing to avoid the subject
with her daughter, Shirley realized that her daughter might be
assuming the worst about her health, and perhaps the truth would
cause her daughter less anxiety.

In weighing the pros and cons of continuing to keep silent
versus having further discussion with her daughter, Shirley decided
that she did want to talk to her daughter in more depth about her
illness. At this point, the social work intern turned to the communication skills Shirley could use to do this, and they practiced with
role plays.

Summary

Motivational interviewing takes into account the level of motivation for change and is designed for those who have not yet committed to action to change problem behavior. The techniques and intervention questions elicit from clients in a nondefensive way the reasons why they should change. The social worker does not advise or tell clients what to do, but rather, using a collaborative process, bolsters motivation so that clients are willing to take action toward their problems.

References

Baer, J., Kivlahan, D., & Donovan, D. (1999). Integrating skills training and motivational therapies. *Journal of Substance Abuse Treatment, 17*(1-2), 15–23.

Burke, B., Arkowitz, H., & Dunn, C. (2002). The efficacy of motivational interviewing and its adaptations: What we know so far. In W. R. Miller and S. Rollnick (Eds.), *Motivational interviewing,* 2nd ed. (pp. 217–250). New York: Guilford.

Carroll, K. (1998). A cognitive-behavioral approach: Treating cocaine addiction. Online: http://www.drugabuse.gov/TXManuals/CBT/CBT1.html. Accessed August 28, 2004.

Connors, G., Donovan, D., & DiClemente, C. (2001). *Substance abuse treatment and the stages of change: Selecting and planning interventions.* New York: Guilford Press.

Dunn, C., Deroo, L., & Rivara, F. (2001). The use of brief interventions adapted from motivational interviewing across behavioral domains: A systematic review. *Addiction, 96,* 1725–1742.

Miller, W., & Rollnick, S. (2002). *Motivational interviewing: Preparing people to change addictive behavior,* 2nd ed. New York: Guilford.

Moyers, T., & Rollnick, S. (2002). A motivational interviewing perspective on resistance in psychotherapy. *JCLP/In Session: Psychotherapy in Practice, 58,* 185–193.

Prochaska, J., & Norcross, J. (1994). *Systems of psychotherapy: A transtheoretical analysis,* 3rd ed. Pacific Grove, CA: Brooks/Cole.

Project MATCH Research Group. (1997). Matching alcoholism treatments to client heterogeneity: Project MATCH posttreatment drinking outcomes. *Journal of Studies On Alcohol, 58,* 7–29.

Project MATCH Research Group. (1998). Matching alcoholism treatments to client heterogeneity: Project MATCH three-year drinking outcomes. *Alcoholism: Clinical & Experimental Research, 22,* 1300–1311.

Walitzer, K., Dermen, K., & Conners, G. (1999). Strategies for preparing clients for treatment: A review. *Behavior Modification, 23*, 129–151.

Yahne, C. E., & Miller, W. R. (1999). Enhancing motivation for treatment and change. In B. S. McCrady and E. E. Epstein (Eds.), *Addictions: A comprehensive guidebook,* (pp. 235–249). New York: Oxford University Press.

APPENDIX

——▼▲▼——

Cognitive-Behavioral Manuals and Resources

Youth Problems

CHILD AND ADOLESCENT ANXIETY[1]

Albano, A. M. (1995). Treatment of social anxiety in adolescents. *Cognitive and Behavioral Practice, 2,* 271–298.

Beidel, D., & Turner, S. (1998). *Shy children, phobic adults: Nature and treatment of social phobia.* Washington, DC: American Psychological Association.

Deblinger, E., & Heflin, A. H. (1996). *Treating sexually abused children and their nonoffending parents: A cognitive-behavioral approach.* Thousand Oaks, CA: Sage.

Hayward, C., Varady, S., Albano, A. M., Thieneman, M., Henderson, L., & Schatzberg, A. F. (2000). Cognitive behavioral group therapy for female socially phobic adolescents: Results of a pilot study. *Journal of the American Academy of Child and Adolescent Psychiatry, 39,* 721–726.

Kearney, C. A., & Albano, A. M. (2000a). *When children refuse school: A cognitive-behavioral therapy approach. Parent workbook.* New York: Psychological Corporation.

Kearney, C. A., & Albano, A. M. (2000b). *When children refuse school: A cognitive-behavioral therapy approach. Therapist's manual.* New York: Psychological Corporation.

Kendall, P. C. (1990). *Coping Cat Workbook.* Ardmore, PA: Workbook.

Kendall, P. C., Kane, M., Howard, B., & Siqueland, L. (1990). *Cognitive-behavioral treatment of anxious children: Treatment manual.* (Available from P. C. Kendall, Department of Psychology, Temple University, Philadelphia, PA 19122).

---

[1] Most of these recommendations come from the following: Velting, O., Setzer, N., & Albano, A. M. (2004). Update on and advances in assessment and cognitive-behavioral treatment of anxiety disorders in children and adolescents. *Professional Psychology: Research and Practice, 35,* 42–54.

March, J., Amaya-Jackson, L., Murray, M., & Schulte, A. (1998). Cognitive-behavioral psychotherapy for children and adolescents with posttraumatic stress disorder after a single-incident stressor. *Journal of the American Academy of Child & Adolescent Psychiatry, 37*, 585–593.

March, J. S., & Mulle, K. (1998). *OCD in children and adolescents: A cognitive-behavioral therapy manual.* New York: Guilford.

Silverman, W. K., & Kurtines, W. M. (1996). *Anxiety and phobic disorders: A pragmatic approach.* New York: Plenum.

ADOLESCENT DEPRESSION

Lewinsohn and Clarke curriculum, Adolescent Coping with Depression Course, is available online: (http://www.kpchr.org/public/acwd/acwd.html).

PARENT TRAINING

Forehand, R., & McMahon, R. J. (1981). *Helping the noncompliant child: A clinician's guide to effective parent training.* New York: Guilford.

Forgatch, M., & Patterson, G. (1989). *Parents and adolescents living together, part 2: Family problem solving.* Eugene, OR: Castalia Publishing.

McNeil, C., Hembree-Kigin, T., & Eyberg, S. (1996). *Short-term play therapy for disruptive children.* King of Prussia, PA: Center for Applied Psychology.

Patterson, G. (1976). *Living with children: New methods for parents and teachers.* Champaign, IL: Research Press.

Patterson, G., & Forgatch, M. (1987). *Parents and adolescents living together: The basics.* Eugene, OR: Castalia Publishing.

Webster-Stratton, C. (1981; revised 2001). *Incredible years parents and children training series.* Retrieved September 2, 2004, from http://www.incredibleyears.com.

PROBLEM-SOLVING SKILLS

Feindler, E., & Ecton, R. (1986). *Adolescent anger control: Cognitive-behavioral techniques.* Elmsford, NY: Pergamon.

Finch, A., Nelson, W., & Ott, E. (1993). *Cognitive-behavioral procedures with children and adolescents: A practical guide.* Needham Heights, MA: Allyn & Bacon.

Shure, M. (1992). *I can problem solve (ICPS): An interpersonal cognitive problem solving program.* Champaign, IL: Research Press.

SOCIAL SKILLS

For a list of social skills training manuals, see Alberg, J., Petry, C., & Eller, A. (1994). *A resource guide for social skills interaction.* Longmont, CO: Sopris West.

General Cognitive-Behavioral

Friedberg, R. (1996). Cognitive-behavioral games and workbooks: Tips for school counselors. *Elementary School Guidance and Counseling, 31,* 11–20.

Adult Problems²

Barlow, D. (2001). *Clinical handbook of psychological disorders: A step-by-step treatment manual,* 3rd ed. New York: Guilford. This book contains detailed treatment guidelines for a number of different problem areas: anxiety (panic disorder and agoraphobia, social anxiety disorder, generalized anxiety disorder, obsessive-compulsive disorder, and posttraumatic stress disorder); substance use disorders (alcohol use disorders and cocaine dependence); depression; borderline personality disorders; sexual dysfunction; couple distress; eating disorders; and bipolar disorder.

DEPRESSION

The following self-help manuals, *Feeling Good* (Burns, 1980) and *Control Your Depression* (Lewinsohn, Munoz, Youngren, & Zeiss, 1986), have been empirically validated, but many other self-help books available have not.

Burns, D. (1999). *Feeling good: The new mood therapy,* rev. ed. New York: Avon.

Lewinsohn, P. M., Munoz, R. F., Youngren, M. A., & Zeiss, A. M. (1986). *Control your depression,* 2nd ed. Englewood Cliffs, NJ: Prentice-Hall.

SUBSTANCE USE DISORDERS

Budney, A. J., & Higgins, S. T. (1998). Therapy manuals for drug addiction: A community reinforcement plus vouchers approach: Treating cocaine addiction. Retrieved on August 18, 2004, from http://www.nida.nih.gov/TXManuals/CRA/CRA1.html.

Carroll, K. (1998). Therapy manuals for drug addiction: A cognitive-behavioral approach: Treating cocaine addiction. Retrieved on August 28, 2004, from http://www.drugabuse.gov/TXManuals/CBT/CBT1.html.

MENTAL RETARDATION

Positive behavior support training curriculum, direct support edition. Available at http://www.aamr.org/Bookstore/.

---

[2] The self-help books listed in this section have been reviewed in Norcross, J., Santrock, J., Campbell, L., Smith, T., Sommer, R., & Zuckerman, E. (2000). *Authoritative guide to self-help resources in mental health.* New York: Guilford.

ASSERTIVENESS

Alberti, R., & Emmons, M. (1991). *Stand up, speak out, talk back*. New York: Pocket Books.
Alberti, R., & Emmons, M. (2001). *Your perfect right: A guide to assertive living*, 8th ed. San Luis Obispo, CA: Impact.
Anthony Bower, S., & Bower, G. (1991). *Asserting yourself: A practical guide for positive change*. Reading, MA: Perseus.
Smith, M. (1975). *When I say no, I feel guilty*. New York: Bantam Books.

RELAXATION

Benson, H. (1975). *The relaxation response*. New York: Morrow.
Benson, H. (1984). *Beyond the relaxation response*. New York: Times Books.
Benson, H., & Stuart, E. (1992). *The wellness book: A comprehensive guide to maintaining health and treating stress-related illness*. New York: Fireside.
Borysenko, J. (1987). *Minding the body, mending the mind*. New York: Bantam Books.
Kabat-Zinn, J. (1994). *Wherever you go, there you are*. New York: Hyperion.
Madders, J. (1997). *The stress and relaxation handbook: A practical guide to self-help techniques*. London, UK: Vermilion.

The Elderly[3]

Dick, L. P., Gallagher-Thompson, D. G., Coon, D. W., Powers, D. V., & Thompson, L. W. (1995). *Cognitive behavioral therapy for late life depression: A client manual*. Palo Alto, CA: VA Palo Alto Health Care System.
Gallagher-Thompson, D., Ossinalde, C., & Thompson, L. W. (1996b). *Como Mantener Su Bienestar*. Palo Alto, CA: VA Palo Alto Health Care System (Spanish Language manual).
Gallagher-Thompson, D., Ossinalde, C., & Thompson, L. W. (1996a). *Coping with caregiving: A class for family caregivers*. Palo Alto, CA: VA Palo Alto Health Care System.
Gallagher-Thompson, D., Rose, J., Florsheim, M., Jacome, P., DelMaestro, S., Peters, L., Gantz, F., Arguello, D., Johnson, C., Mooreland, R. S., Polich, T. M., Chesney, M., & Thompson, L. W. (1992). *Controlling your frustration: A class for caregivers*. Palo Alto, CA: VA Palo Alto Health Care System.
Thompson, L., Gallagher, D., & Lovett, S. (1992). *Increasing life satisfaction class: Leaders' and participant manuals*. Palo Alto, CA: Department of Veterans Affairs Medical Center and Stanford University.

---

[3] The following references are from Laidlaw, K., Thompson, L., Gallagher-Thompson, D., & Dick-Siskin, L. (2003). *Cognitive behavior therapy with older people*. West Sussex, UK: John Wiley.

Thompson, L. W., Gallagher-Thompson, D., & Dick, L. P. (1995). *Cognitive behavioural therapy for late life depression: A therapist manual.* Palo Alto, CA: Older Adult and Family Center, Veterans Affairs Palo Alto Health Care System.

Thompson, L. W., Gallagher, D., Laidlaw, K., & Dick, L. P. (2000). *Cognitive behavioral therapy for late life depression: A therapist manual.* UK Version. Edinburgh, UK: University of Edinburgh, Dept of Psychiatry.*

---

*A copy of this manual is available on request by writing to Ken Laidlaw, University of Edinburgh, Department of Psychiatry, Kennedy Tower, Royal Edinburgh Hospital, Morningside Park, Edinburgh, EH10 5HF. For all other manuals, please write to Dr. Dolores Gallagher-Thompson, Professor of Research, Department of Psychiatry and Behavioral Sciences, Stanford University School of Medicine, California.

Index

————— ▼▲▼ —————